Hi

Subtitle: Who is God?
Handbook and Study Guide

by Maralyn B. Dyck

Edited by Peter H. Dyck

Copyright 2015 © Maralyn B. Dyck

Unless otherwise indicated, all Scripture quotations are taken from the Holy Bible, New Living Translation, copyright © 1996. Used by permission of Tyndale House Publishers, Inc., Wheaton, Illinois 60189. All rights reserved.

Web site: www.biblemapsplus.com

Published May 22, 2016

PREFACE

This book is not a theological treatise. The first three chapters provide a doctrinal and historical foundation.

Early in the book I introduce some solid teaching for new believers in knowing and understanding God. I have attempted to answer many questions that doubters or new Christians might ask.

This is followed by the actions taken by God including creation and the universal flood.

It is designed to be used as a Handbook and Study Guide, allowing spaces for writing notes, adding illustrations or jotting down questions to research.

Maralyn Dyck

ACKNOWLEDGEMENTS

How can I begin to express my thanks and gratitude to all those who have helped and encouraged me during the writing of this book?

I would especially like to thank my favorite editor, my beloved husband, Peter.

Thank you Corrie for the wonderful cover.

I would also like to thank all my family and friends who have been so patient with me while I have ignored them from time to time while putting this book together. Without the support and comments from all of you this book would probably never have come together.

A LETTER TO MY READERS

This book has been designed to work as a handbook and reference guide for pastors and Christian workers. It also is designed to be simplified enough for reading straight through as a book for those who want to know more about God and how we can relate to Him both as a loving Father and a Savior. It gives guidance on many issues with the Holy Bible as the final authority.

For the skeptics, atheists and agnostics

No doubt you think yourself secure in your beliefs and lifestyles and have no desire to change. That is your choice. However, should you dare to read this book, one of three things may happen: 1) you may get a good laugh, 2) you may find many of your beliefs challenged or 3) you just might learn some truths that will turn your whole life around. The risk is yours.

For the doubters and new Christians

I am praying and trusting that this book will help to open your eyes to see what an awesome God we have and through the process learn what it takes to know God spiritually, not just with the intellect, but with the heart. Within these pages you will find out how to find peace and happiness in the midst of trials and persecutions.

For the wounded and God-seekers

Those who sense emptiness in their lives need something more, something that is real. I feel the first step is to get to know who God is and understand what His plans for His people include. The first three chapters of the book deal exclusively with getting to know God and include some of the questions you may be asking yourself about God. The fourth chapter tells what God has done, followed by His plan for your life in chapter 5.

For mature Christians

By reading this book you may glean some new truths and strengthen your faith in God. This book could prove to be a reference manual when dealing with people in your families or ministries. I trust you will enjoy reading it as much as I have enjoyed putting it together.

Table of Contents

CHAPTER 1— Who IS God? 13
Knowing and Understanding God 13
   Introduction 13
   Address: 15
   Phone Number: 15
What is the Holy Bible? 16
   Point of interest—Bible Numerics 9, 10 18
God's Attributes 21
   1) Omnipresent—Present everywhere 21
   2) Omniscient—Knows all things 22
   3) Omnipotent—All-powerful 22
   4) Sovereign 23
   5) Unchangeable 23
   6) Eternal—No beginning and no ending; He is NOT finite. 23
   References by Leading Men in the Bible 24
   Summary 27
What is the Trinity? 28
   How can God be three separate persons and still be one God? 28
   God, the Father 29
      Names of God 29
      Eight Attributive or Qualifying Names: 31
   God, the Son 33
      Names of Jesus Christ: 33
   God, the Holy Spirit 36
      Names of the Holy Spirit: 36
   Summary 37
CHAPTER 2—Answering Some of the Major Questions 41

Why is God silent when we desperately need Him? 41
Getting to Know God While He is Silent 42
Hearing from God 43
Dream One 44
Dream Two 45
Should God always rescue us? 48
What is sin? 49
Why did God allow Sin and Evil to enter a perfect world? 51
CHAPTER 3—"In the Beginning God..." 55
How did the world begin? 55
Pre Creation Period 56
Refuting Revolution 56
Creation Week 57
Day One 57
Day Two 58
Day Three 58
Day Four 60
Day Five 60
Point of interest! 60
Day Six 61
Summary of Day Six 63
Point of Interest 63
Day Seven 64
For what purpose did God create man? 66
What did God create when He created man in God's image? 66
The Body—World-consciousness 66
Point of Interest 67
The Soul—Self-consciousness 67
The Spirit—God-consciousness 67

The Fall of Man 69

Who is Lucifer? 71

Do you have something against God? 72

How can we recognize Satan? 74

Why were animal sacrifices necessary? 77

What reciprocated the first murder? 78

Where did Cain get his wife? 79

    Traditional View 79

    Second View 80

    Third View 80

    Summary 81

Chapter 4—Degeneration and Destruction of Mankind 85

    Who was Noah? 85

    The Universal Flood 86

    A new beginning 87

    Tower of Babel 87

    Point of Interest 88

Chapter 5—God's Plan of Salvation 100

    Eternal Life 100

    Union with God—Not Separation 100

    God's Remedy is the Cross 100

    Man's Response is to Receive Christ 101

    Prayer of Commitment 101

    Where Do I Go From Here? 101

    FOLLOWING ARE SOME SCRIPTURES TO HELP YOU: 102

REFERENCES 103

RECOMMENDED READING 106

Chapter One

Who Is God?

The Silken Fabric

By Patricia R. Miller

Our most painful wounds will frequently come
When the Holy Spirit is soaring in our soul.
The destroyer slashes down the silken fabric
of the anointing
As it flows in a crescendo of joy!
It shatters the spirit and leaves a searing,
bleeding wound.
But as the eagle lies prostrate before the sun
To bring healing to wounds, raw and tender
Now we lie quietly before our God
And allow the Son to bring healing
So that we may soar again…
Stronger and higher than ever before!

CHAPTER 1— Who IS God?

Astronomers discover a new universe with a bright star in the center. God has promised us a new heaven and a new earth when

He returns for His church, the believers. Revelations 21:1-8

Knowing and Understanding God

Introduction

Definition: God is a spirit or ghost; a ghost has no flesh, bones or blood[17]. In Luke 24:39 Jesus says, "…ghosts don't have bodies…" God has always existed and is eternal in nature. He will exist forever.

Everything that exists has been created by Him, including time, matter, energy and the universes. There is no other God!

God can create thousands of people to worship Him, but He did not want robots. He wanted a people who would choose to worship Him and serve Him, a people who could fellowship with Him, rule and reign with Him over the universes for eternity. That is where we, the people of earth enter the scene. God created our universe and earth specifically for us.

We are His chosen people; now it is up to us to choose Him. If we do, we will join Him for eternity in a new and exciting life where there is no more sorrow, illness, grief or death! Read what God has to say:

"I heard a voice shout from the throne; God's home is now with his people. He will live with them, and they will be his own. Yes, God will make his home among his people. He will wipe all tears from their eyes, and there will be no more death, suffering, crying, or pain. These things of the past are gone forever...I am making everything new..My words are true and can be trusted. Everything is finished!

"I am Alpha and Omega, the beginning and he end. I will freely give water from the life-giving fountain to everyone who is thirsty. All who win the victory will be given these blessings. I will be their God and they will be my people.

But I will tell you what will happen to cowards and to everyone who is unfaithful or dirty-minded or who murders or is sexually immoral or uses witchcraft or worships idols or tells lies. They will be thrown into that lake of fire and burning sulphur. This is the second death."

God is a God of LOVE for those who obey him, honor him and give their lives over to him as his followers. However, God is a God of JUSTICE for those who refuse to obey him and give their lives to him, by turning away from all evil and sin.

It is a choice! Every person on earth has the right to make their own choice. God designed everything to that end. He wants people who will turn their backs on evil and start living a life that is honorable to him. That does not mean we have to be perfect; we are flesh and will fail him from time to time, but he forgives everyone who **genuinely** asks for forgiveness.

God knows our hearts; you cannot fool God, so don't even try. If you ask for forgiveness with plans to continue as you are, living in sin, your "confessions" to him will not help you. NO SIN is too great that God will not forgive you.

With God everything is **provisional**. You do what God expects of you, you will be forgiven. Every time you stumble and fall, get back up again and ask forgiveness again. There is no limit on God's forgiveness as long as you are genuinely seeking God and doing your best to obey and follow him. You will have eternal life with him if you follow him. You will join Satan and his evil angels in the lake of fire for eternity if you do not..YOUR CHOICE!

I cannot emphasize this enough! Live forever with God or with Satan. Believers and non-believers alike will face the throne of God's judgment.

Are you prepared to face God and answer for the things you have been doing with your life?

Remember, nothing is hidden from God. He knows your every thought and every action. You will have to account for everything you do or think. Believers are forgiven for all their bad deeds and will be rewarded according to the good deeds they have done for God; non-believers are punished according to their own actions.

This book will provide you with further insights into who God is and what life is all about. It will also provide helps and suggestions as you seek to learn more about God and what is expected of believers.

Address:

Everywhere. You cannot find a place where God is not always present; His presence is always with us, even when we can't feel or sense His presence.

Phone Number:

Instant voice contact - just talk to God and He will hear you and commune with you. You just have to learn how to listen.

Notes:

What is the Holy Bible?

The Bible or Holy Bible, also known as the Holy Scriptures or the Word of God, is the history of God's dealings with His people since the creation of the universes to the end times when Jesus Christ returns for His bride.

The Bible is a collection of sacred writings, which are divided into two sections known as the "Old Testament" and the "New Testament."

The Holy Bible is regarded as the depository and authoritative divine record of God's revelation of Himself and of His will to the fathers by the prophets, and through His Son, Jesus Christ, to the church of a later age.

It includes both fulfilled prophecies and prophecies still to be fulfilled before Jesus Christ comes back for the believers, His church, who will become part of His bride for eternity.

Each Person of the Trinity has unique names that scripture uses when referring to them.

Since the Father is a Person, He can enter into a personal relationship with each one of us. The closest and most tender love is that of the Father. In Matthew 6:8 we read, "...your Father knows exactly what you need even before you ask Him."

This was also seen very clearly in God's relationship to His covenant people, Israel. However, their relationship with God was more of a collective one, as a nation, rather than a personal one. See Psalm 68:5; Exodus 4:22.

There is a redemptive relationship through Jesus Christ that applies to ALL believers. In the context of redemption, it is viewed from two aspects, that of their standing in Christ and that of the regenerating work of the Holy Spirit.

The Father wants us to be His sons and daughters and desires that we love and worship only Him and obey Him in all things.

The Father's love is unconditional; but for the relational kind of love, we must walk in obedience. His love for us does not rule out discipline, but rather demands it, just as a wayward child has to be disciplined.

A father needs to be sensitive to his children's needs both physically and spiritually; he also needs to know when to put his foot down and administer discipline for wrongdoing—and the right way to do it! Children need to feel loved, needed and understood even when being disciplined.

This is the kind of relationship we can have with our heavenly Father. II Corinthians 6:18 reads, "And I will be your Father, and you will be my sons and daughters, says the Lord Almighty."

Many of you have not had a good father-child relationship. Perhaps you have lived with an absentee father or perhaps you are an orphan or a foster child, so it is harder for you to understand the concept I am presenting here.

From The Heart of George MacDonald we read, "In my own childhood and boyhood my father was the refuge from all the ills of life, even sharp pain itself. Therefore I say to son or daughter who has no pleasure in the name Father, 'You must interpret the word by all that you have missed in life. All that human tenderness can give or desire in the nearness and readiness of love, all and infinitely more must be true of the perfect Father—of the maker of fatherhood.' "[2]

Each one of you has the right to choose God. No one can do it for you. If you choose God, nothing can take you out of His hands - not even death.

Absence from the earth leads you into the presence of God in heaven. What a wonderful and encouraging thought! The Father has His eye upon us at all times. He is present with us even when we cannot feel it.

The Father is patient and understanding, but He will not tolerate sin. He will forgive you over and over again without condemnation as long as your repentance is sincere.

No sin is too big or too terrible that he will not forgive you if you ask him to do so. This unusual photo is called "The Eye of God." by Nassau

We cannot fool God! He knows our hearts; God knows when our repentance is genuine. God understands our frailty and the fact that we sin over and over again, even when we do not want to do so. See Romans 7:14-25.

Only one Person born on earth did not sin; that Person was Jesus Christ, the Son of God.

The Bible says that if you commit one sin, you are guilty of all sins in the eyes of the Father. See James 2:10.

That is why the Father sent His only Son to earth—to take our sins and place them upon His own Son's shoulders. This will be explained more fully in the next section on The Son.

The relationship between God and man is that of a father and his sons and daughters. It is not a master/slave relationship! This relationship between God and man demonstrates a true, ideal relationship with God. It is as a Father that He hears us and answers our prayers, considering them and answering them, as a Father should do.

Point of interest—Bible Numerics 9, 10

Note: Every Hebrew and Greek letter had a numerical value as well as an alphabetical value, as they did not represent numbers with a separate numerical symbol like we do today. It was these numbers that Dr. Panin used in his study. There is nothing mystical about them at all. Dr. Panin's works were just plain mathematics. Anyone can check it out for him or herself.

There are many Biblical evidences of the authenticity of the Bible and that it is indeed the divinely inspired Word of God. Bible Numerics is one evidence outside the pages of the Bible that, when added to all the other evidence, helps to prove the inspiration of the Bible.

This view has nothing to do with numerology and there is nothing mystical about it. It is just mathematics at its best.

Within the pages of the Bible there is no mention of the underlying mathematical structure of the Bible, but it is there nevertheless.

What you do with it or think about it is up to you.

Dr. Ivan Panin spent 50 years of his life working with Biblical Numerics. His original works were hand-penned on 43,000 detailed pages of analysis! His works were called Bible Numerics.

There are some phenomenal mathematical designs underlying both the Greek text of the New Testament and the Hebrew text of the Old Testament. Hebrew and Greek are two languages that also use their alphabet as their numbering system.

In the early 1900's Dr. Panin offered $100 (a lot of money in those days) to anyone who could write even one paragraph of 300 words which would reflect this same numerical phenomenon. Apparently, not one entry was received.

Every letter, word, phrase, sentence, sub-paragraph, paragraph, section and book takes on a definite arithmetical sum and system. To remove or change even one letter would destroy the numerical patterns existing throughout the texts.

The original Hebrew manuscript was written in one long string of letters with a space between each letter. There were no words, sentences or paragraphs!

Some of the manuscripts were written in Aramaic and translated into Hebrew. This left the translation of the original manuscript to the work of a scholar.

The true original manuscripts were never located, just parts or portions of copies that had been handed down through the centuries; these had to be put together, much like doing a giant jigsaw puzzle – the result being the current translation of the Old Testament.

What method could be used to determine the actual content of the Old Testament and the accuracy of the Old Testament?

Dr. Ivan Panin looked for a way to prove what should be included and what should not. He wanted to write a translation that was absolutely accurate—a major task, since he had to go all the way back to all the portions of manuscripts available and sort them out. Bible Numerics proved to him to be a helpful tool.

The same situation applied to the New Testament – many writers, many letters, some not originally written in Greek, but later translated into Greek. There were many opportunities for error.

Again Bible Numerics proved to him to be a method of testing the manuscript pieces to determine which ones were authentic and which ones were spurious.

One of the results of this work was a translation of the New Testament called "The New Testament from the Greek text as established by Bible Numerics." It was first printed in 1914 and has become widely known as a research tool and has been used by many scholars and theologians to this very day.

I have a copy of this New Testament, the 1966 edition. It is a very interesting translation—a very literal translation. He didn't try to make smooth flowing English sentences for the benefit of the reader. He did not add any alternative translations. since **they** did not fit the mathematical pattern!

As is always the case with any translation, there are many who oppose and many who approve. However, has anyone else come up with a better way to determine the accuracy of the original manuscripts?

The recurrence of the number 7 or an exact multiple of 7, -in the original, is found throughout the Bible and is widely recognized. They demonstrate an intricacy of design that testifies to a supernatural origin! The Bible is the inspired Word of God or it is not. If you believe that it is, then you must believe all the things written in it; e.g. in Bible Numerics there are some interesting facts about Genesis 1:1

Example:

The entire first verse has 7 words (In the oldest Hebrew sample available) e.g.

There are 28 letters (7 x 4)

The three leading nouns in the verse (God, heaven, and earth) have a numeric value of 777.

Their place value sum is 147 (7 x 7 x 3).

There are many more elaborate mathematical constructions in this first verse, all using the number 7.[10]

God's Attributes

Definition: Means an inherent characteristic or a word ascribing a quality.[17]

1) Omnipresent—Present everywhere

God is everywhere at one and the same time. There is no place on earth or in all the universes where man can hide from God.

He is with each one of us ALL the time. He never leaves us stranded or alone. Rather, it is we who turn our backs on God and render him ineffective in our lives. **God will not force us to love and obey Him**. He is still there beside us **but leaves us to our own devices until we ask Him to come into our lives**.

In Jeremiah 23:23-24 the Lord asks Jeremiah several questions. God is amazed at the naiveté of humans, that they actually think that He cannot see what they are doing! He follows his questions with the statement that He is everywhere in all the heavens and earth.

In one of King Solomon's prayers he states that even the highest heavens cannot contain Him, much less the Temple that he built for Him! See I Kings 8:27.

In Psalms 139:1-12 King David had a lot to say about God. He states that God has examined his heart and knows everything about him; God knows his every thought no matter where he is. God charts his path and tells him where to stop and rest. Every moment God knows where he is and what he is going to say even before he says it; God precedes him and also follows him. He places His hand of blessing on David's head.

David pauses, then says, "Such knowledge is too wonderful for me, too great for me to know." Then David begins again. He states that he can never escape from God's spirit! He can never get away from His presence!

"If I go up to heaven, you are there; if I go down to the place of the dead, you are there. If I ride the wings of the morning, if I dwell by the farthest oceans, even there your hand will guide me, and your strength will support me." David goes on to say that he cannot even hide in the darkness, that darkness and light are both the same to God.

To put it more plainly, there is **nowhere** we can hide from the presence of God, not even in space. His presence is everywhere! But who wants to hide from God? Not me! To me it is a real comfort to know I have access to God anywhere and at any time.

Constant communion with God is the key to a better relationship with God, a relationship that brings fulfillment, a win-win combination.

2) Omniscient—Knows all things

God knows your every thought and action. Nothing is hidden from God. God knows your heart, who you are and what you are. You cannot fool or deceive God! Just yourself, and sometimes other people! God knows ALL the past, present and future. God knows every choice we make and everything that will happen as a result of those choices.

The Bible says that " the eyes of the Lord search the whole earth in order to strengthen those whose hearts are fully committed to him." II Chronicles 16:9a

We also read that "The Lord knows people's thoughts…" Psalm 94:11a.

Daniel praises God and states that only God has **all wisdom** and power. See Daniel 2:20.

We need to guard our hearts and minds! Claiming ignorance will not protect us; full repentance will.

3) Omnipotent—All-powerful

God must be all-powerful. To lack this He definitely could not be God; God can do the impossible; God performs miracles. God created the heavens and the universes, the earth and everything upon the earth; God created mankind in His own image. No other god exists. See Genesis 1:1.

A psalmist says that when God spoke, the world began, that it appeared at His command. Read Psalm 33.

In Job 42:2 Job says that God can do anything, that no one can stop him. God created everything that exists…time, space, matter, and energy.

This includes physics, the law of physics, biology and chemistry.

4) Sovereign

God makes His own plans and carries them out in *His own time and way*. This is an expression of His supreme intelligence, power, authority and wisdom. God is Lord of heaven and earth.

Isaiah states that God's ever expanding peaceful government will never end. This means that we will live peacefully with God for all eternity.

5) Unchangeable

God is so constituted that He cannot change. This refers to the **character** of God, *not the mind of God*. God's character is absolute.

God created all the planets and stars which are constantly changing. James tells us God is not like the lights in the heavens, because God **never changes** or casts moving shadows. See James 1:17

6) Eternal—No beginning and no ending; He is NOT finite.

God has no beginning and no ending. Idols and pagan gods are made by people and have a beginning. Satan was created, so he had a beginning.

There is only *one* true God.

In Psalm 90:2 Moses states that God is without beginning or ending.

In Rev. 1:8 John quotes the Lord, "I am...the Almighty One."

As humans we have a beginning, but we will have no ending; we will have eternal life. Those who refuse to believe in Jesus and repent from their sins will also have eternal existence **with Satan** and his demons in a lake of fire that never consumes and never stops burning—an eternal lake of fire.

The choice is ours, one we must make before we die. None of us know when we are going to die, so it is imperative we make the right choice **now**—later will be too late.

References by Leading Men in the Bible

1) King David—Second king of Israel (circa 1055BC)

In the book of Psalms many prayers and songs of King David are recorded. He mentions many of God's attributes. God is righteous, just, merciful, glorious, longsuffering, compassionate and gracious, unsearchable, good, upright and benevolent. The references for these attributes are: Psalms 25:8; 86:5, 15; 100:5; 103:5, 8; 119:68; 145:3, 5, 12, 17.

2) Ezra—An expert in the Law of God (688-458BC)

King Nebuchadnezzar deported Israel as a nation to Babylon. Seventy years later Ezra led a group of them back to their homeland, Israel.

As an expert in the Law of God, he helped the people reorganize their religious and social life in order to safeguard the spiritual heritage of Israel. Ezra shows God to be communicative and in his conversation with God he calls him just. See Ezra 6:22b; 7:27-28; 9:15.

3) In Various Historical Records

In various historical records God is called holy, compassionate, gracious and great, to name just a few. See I Samuel 2:2; I Kings 8:23; II Chronicles 2:5.

4) Isaiah—A great prophet (circa 740BC–681BC)

In his book Isaiah tells us God is holy, glorious and true, also that He is light. See Isaiah 2:10, 19; 6:3; 60:19-20; 65:16.

5) Jeremiah—A great prophet (circa 627BC - 586BC)

Jeremiah has been called the "weeping prophet," as he loved his people dearly and grieved at having to be the one to pronounce God's judgment upon them. He lived a long time, long enough to see many of his own prophecies fulfilled. Jeremiah called God the true

God, the living God and the eternal King. He also called God mighty and great. See Jeremiah 10:6, 10; 12:1

6) Job—A godly rich man whom Satan tried to destroy

In the book of Job it says God is unsearchable, immortal and invisible. See Job 11:7; 23:8, 9.

7) John—Disciple of Jesus (circa 25 – 28AD)

John stayed with Jesus during His years of ministry on earth. During his final years John was exiled to the island of Patmos where he wrote the book of Revelation. In his writings he called God holy, love and light – the light of the world. John 1; 3:16; 16:27; I John 1:5; 4:9; Revelations 15:4

8) Luke – A physician and historian (circa 29AD)

Luke wrote to Theophilus telling him about the ministry of Jesus. In a follow-up letter he gives a report on Jesus' disciples, apostles and the Holy Spirit. Luke was often with Paul; historians believe he possibly ministered to Paul as a physician while he was in prison. Luke called Jesus holy. Since Jesus is part of the Godhead, that means Luke called God holy. See Acts 3:27

9) Matthew – A tax collector (circa 25 - 28AD)

Matthew became one of the twelve disciples of Jesus.

In Matthew 7:11 he wrote of the Father, "…how much more will your heavenly Father give good gifts to those who ask Him!" NAS God is benevolent.

10) Moses—Israelite leader and first Bible historian (circa 1576-1456BC)

Moses was raised in the royal palace of Pharaoh in Egypt. At the age of forty he killed an Egyptian who was fighting with an Israelite. Fearing that Pharaoh would find out and have him killed, Moses fled into the desert where he married and lived peacefully for forty years as a shepherd.

At the age of eighty God called Moses to lead the Israelites out of Egypt where they were in bondage. Moses, in his obedience to his supernatural encounter with God returned to Egypt and confronted Pharaoh with God's command, "Let my people go!"

As the first historian, Moses wrote the Pentateuch, or Torah, of the Old Testament and had a great deal to say about God. In his writings Moses called God **holy, faithful, longsuffering, compassionate, gracious, unique—one of a kind, the only true God**. See Exodus 15:11; 34:6; Numbers 14:18; Deuteronomy 4:31; 7:9; 32:4; 33:26

11) Nahum—A prophet from Elkosh (circa 663-612BC)

In his writing Nahum refers to God as "**jealous and avenging**." Nahum 1:2

12) Nehemiah—Cupbearer to the Persian King, Artaxerxes I (465 to 425 BC)

Nehemiah speaks of the **benevolence of God**. In Nehemiah 9:20-25 he outlines all the good things that God provided for the Israelite people during their forty years in the wilderness.

13) Paul—An apostle of Jesus Christ (circa 48-67AD)

Paul was a zealous member of the Pharisee party. His first appearance in Jerusalem was as a persecutor of Christians. Paul's remarkable conversion turned him around, and he became a strong follower of Jesus Christ. He mentored many young men and was an apostle to many of the young churches springing up everywhere. His main ministry was to the Gentiles, since the Jews did not accept him but threatened to kill him.

He wrote many letters to these young churches and these letters are included in the New Testament, where they are called "books." In his writings Paul calls God **holy, righteous, just, faithful, merciful, unsearchable, incorruptible, a consuming fire, immortal** and **invisible** to name just a few.

See I Corinthians 6:16; I Timothy 1:17; II Timothy 2:13; Romans 1:23; 9:18; 11:33; Hebrews 1:8, 13a; and 12:29.

14) Peter—Disciple of Jesus

Peter wrote two books in the New Testament. In I Peter 1:16 he calls God **holy**.

15) Unknown Psalmist—Someone saved from death.

In Psalm 116 this psalmist calls God **righteous**, **just**, **compassionate**, **gracious**, **great**. Read the whole Psalm!

The above list is not by any means exhaustive. There are many more character references in the Bible.

Summary

God provided a means of redemption so that a **just** and **holy** God could also show **love** and **mercy**. There is no evil in God; He is a God of **love** and **tender kindness**; He wants what is best for us; He will not force anything upon us. We are God's creation! We belong to him!

There are going to be times when we **think** that one or more of the qualifications of God do not seem to apply. Many people have an unbalanced view of God. Some over emphasize His love and forget that He is just and holy at the same time.

Others only see God as a God of vengeance and judgment, a God to be feared, even hated, forgetting that God is also loving and merciful.

While the holiness and justice of God demand that sin must be punished, ***His love compels Him to forgive sin and show mercy to repentant sinners***, made possible because of Jesus' sacrifice—redemption that allows forgiveness and mercy.

Apostle Paul reminds us that the wages of sin is death, but the free gift of God is eternal life through Christ Jesus our Lord. See Romans 6:23.

Notes:

What is the Trinity?

How can God be three separate persons and still be one God?

"God" is plural, not singular, in the Hebrew language. The Trinity is God manifested in three Persons, the Father, the Son and the Holy Spirit, as to function and office. The Lord our God is ONE God in contrast to the plurality of pagan gods. See Deuteronomy 6:4; Isaiah 44:6; 45:21

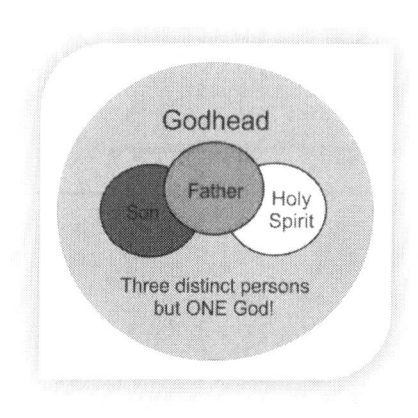

There is a mystery here that cannot be understood or defined by us. Our finite human minds cannot get around the complexity of the Trinity (or Godhead). We do not have to understand it in order to believe it; God says it is so, and we have to take His word for it. There is no other way for us to understand as long as we are here on earth.

The Christian faith believes that there is only one God, one divine nature and being. This One Being is tripartite (three Persons) known as the Father, the Son and the Holy Spirit. These three Persons are joint partakers of the same nature and majesty of God. For example John Smith is a father, a husband and a carpenter to different people. At the same time he is still just one man, John Smith. One main difference is that the three Persons of the Trinity are able to work separately **at the same time.**

Thus, the mystery.

When Jesus the Son was baptized, the Father spoke from heaven, and the Holy Spirit descended from heaven in the form of a dove. See Luke 3:21-22.

All three Persons of the Trinity were present and working at the time of the creation of the world and mankind. See Genesis 1; John 1.

Let's take a closer look at each Person of the Trinity in order to better understand the way God works in our lives.

God, the Father
Names of God

International Standard Bible Encylopaedia.[17]

Note: This list is just a summary and does not include ALL the names. However, the main ones are given. Further study on any subject in this book would be very beneficial and is highly recommended. The Hebrew and Greek names have been transliterated, i.e. using roughly the English equivalent spelling.

1 Jehovah Exodus 3:14; 6:2-4; 34:5-7; Psalm 102

Main Name God is a spirit or ghost; a ghost has no flesh, bones or blood. In Luke 24:39 Jesus says, "...ghosts don't have bodies..." This name became Israel's distinctive name for the Deity of Israel. Used in Exodus 3:13-14 as "I will be what I will be"...say..."'I WILL BE' hath sent me." Also used as "HE WILL BE." This is the closest meaning that has been understood.

In the New Testament the name **"I AM THAT I AM"** is closely related to this name. **"YHWH"** is also used with basically the same meaning.

This was a description of who He is when Moses is to speak to the people on His behalf. The name of the Deity given here is similar to that of "Jehovah," except that it is more personal since He is speaking of Himself indicating His covenant pledge to be with and for Israel in all the ages to follow.

2 Elohim Genesis 1:12; Deuteronomy 10:17; Psalm 68

Means "might" or "power". Used to express "majesty," creator" or "all-mightiness." It is a generic term rather than a specific personal name for the Deity.

3 Eloah

Seems to mean "to be strong," used in poetry such as in Job and Psalms.

4 El, Allah

Seems to infer "to be strong", "the all powerful One," "creator" or "in front of." It is used mostly in Job and the Psalms.

5 Adhon, Adhonay, Adoni Psalm 8; Isaiah 40:3-5; Ezekiel 16:8

Can mean "my great Lord" or "the Lord." Generally used as a personal name.

6 Rock

Used as a title of God. It represents that God is steadfast and a safe retreat.

7 Kadhosh

Means **"Holy One"** as in the "Holy One" of Israel. It shows his peculiar and unchanging covenant-relationship to Israel.

8 Shadday, "Almighty"

As in "to terrify." God is manifested by the terribleness of His mighty acts.

9. El Shaddai

"All Sufficient One," "God of Mountains," and "God Almighty."

10. YHWY Exodus 3:14; Malachi 3:6

"Self Existent One" See **1 Jehovah**.

11. J, Jehovah-Rapha Exodus 15:25-27; Psalm 103:3; 147:3

"Lord Who Heals."

12. Jehovah-Rohi Psalm 23:1-3; Isaiah 53:6

"My Shepherd."

13. Jehovah-Tsidkenu Jeremiah 23:5-6; 33:16; Ezekiel 36:26-27

"Our Righteousness."

Eight Attributive or Qualifying Names:

1 Abhir, "Mighty One"

It is always combined with Israel or Jacob. It has to do with divine strength, "to be strong." Jacob was the first one to use this name.

2 El-Elohe-Israel

The name "El" is combined with a number of descriptive adjectives to represent God in His various attributes.

3 Elyon, "Most High"

Means "to go up." It is used of persons or things to indicate their elevation or exaltation. Such as, "Exalted One," who is lifted far above all gods and men. Points to a high conception of Deity.

4 Gibbor, "Mighty [One]"

The Hebrew thought of His God as fighting for Him, making this title apply to His God. He was the Mighty Man of war.

5 El-Roi

"The God who sees me." Literally, "of sight." eg God saw Hagar in her plight when she was fleeing from Sarah's persecution.

6 Caddik, "Righteous"

One of the covenant attributes of God. Means to be straight or right.

7 Kanna, "Jealous"

Did not bear the evil meaning as we know it now but it meant "righteous zeal," Jehovah's name for His own zeal and glory.

8 Cebha'-oth, "Lord of Hosts"

It is used of heavenly bodies and earthly forces; of the army of Israel; of the Heavenly beings. The title is probably intended to include *all* created agencies and beings.

The variety of names which characterizes the Old Testament is lacking in the New Testament. Many correspond to several in the Old Testament. Some of these are "**Lord of lords**," "**King of kings**, "**Father**," "**Master**," "**Shepherd**," and "**Potentate**."

Only two not mentioned above are listed below:[17]

1 Kurios, "Lord"

In each case when this name is used there is evident emphasis on sovereignty and corresponds to the "Adhon" of the Old Testament.

2 Theos, "God"

In its true sense it expresses essential Deity, and when used in this way is applied to Christ and to the Father. It corresponds to the name of Elohim of the Old Testament.

3 Descriptive and Figurative Names

"Highest" and "Most High" which correspond to "Elyon" and "Shadday" of the Old Testament. See the Old Testament names above.

Notes:

God, the Son

God, the Son has many names. I am listing some of them:

Names of Jesus Christ:

1 Emmanuel/Immanual Isaiah 7:14-8:8; Matthew 1L23; John 1:18
"Only begotten Son of God."

2 King of Kings Matthew. 2:2; 21:5; Luke 8:24; Revelation 19:16
King over all other kings.

3--Lord of Lords Revelations 19:16; I Timothy 6:15
Lord over all other lords. Jesus is Lord. (See King of Kings)

4--Messiah Daniel 9:25; John 1:41, 4:25
Jesus is the Messiah. Jesus is Christ, the Anointed One.

5 Wonderful Counselor Isaiah 9:6; I John 2:1; John 14:16; Luke 2:25
This means He is our "defense attorney" before God, the Father, Advocate, Comforter, Consolation of Israel, Intercessor, Mediator, Paraclete.

6 Almighty Revelations 1:8; Isaiah 9:6; Psalm 24:8; I Timothy 6:15
"All powerful"

7 Everlasting Father Isaiah 9:6; John 1:1-3
"Is forever"

8 Prince of Peace Isaiah 9:6; Ephesians 2:14; Hebrews 7:1-2
"Our Peace"

9 Redeemer Job 19:25l; Ruth 2:14; Matthew 20:28; I Timothy 2:6

"Our Redemption"

10 Son of God Luke 1:35; Hebrews 4:14; John 1:14; Luke 1:32

Son of God by nature.

The Son is the second Person of the Godhead. Since Jesus Christ is also a Person, we can have a personal relationship with him. As part of the Godhead, He was present when the world and the heavens were created. Read John 1.

The Son had another very important mission to perform. The Son was to be the means of redemption for mankind. The ungodliness of mankind prevented mankind from entering the presence of the Father.

The Father's love for us required Him to find a way for mankind to become holy and righteous in His sight. The holiness and justice of God demanded it.

God found a way of redemption for mankind that satisfies both the love of God and the holiness of God.

This way satisfied the Law, yet left man with a free will to choose his own destiny—hell or heaven, damnation or salvation.

Jesus Christ was and is and always will be the answer. The Father sent His only Son to be born of a virgin. His human name was to be Jesus. Jesus is the only answer to life's questions.

In Cry Joy we read, "The poor flocked to Jesus, hoping against hope He could change their miserable fortunes for the better. They knew they had great needs and there seemed to be no one else they could turn to for help. Jesus healed their diseases, raised their dead, and soothed their broken hearts. More than this He reminded them that God had not forgotten them, that even in their poverty they could be elevated to the status of children of God if only they would have faith. Many received His words as assurance from God that, at least in the long run, justice and mercy would prevail."[1]

As both God and man, Jesus' first work was to minister to the Israelites* and reveal the Father to them; this Jesus did. To this end Jesus taught and performed miracles all through the period of His ministry.

*The Israelites were descendants of Jacob, whose name God changed to Israel when he had a true change of heart to live for God. Jacob's twelve sons and their descendants became known as the twelve tribes of Israel, or corporately, just as Israel.

One strong impression of Jesus' ministry was that of **authority**. Jesus had the authority to forgive sins and to heal the broken-hearted, the sick and the lame.

At the time of the crucifixion and resurrection, Jesus took from Satan the authority over the earth that he had stolen from Adam. At that time Jesus did not destroy Satan or remove his current power.

What he did do was remove Satan's authority over the earth and over us. Through Jesus we have received our authority back again, and in His name we have the authority over the spiritual realm, in *our sphere of influence*.

The final work of Jesus Christ was redemptive. The Father sent Him to be a sacrifice for the redemption of mankind.

While on the cross, Jesus took upon himself all the past, present and future sins of the whole human race. **Jesus died that we might live.**

Now the holiness of the Father can look upon us through the spilled blood of Jesus Christ, His Son, and see us as righteous and holy in His sight.

Jesus rose from the dead on the third day thus setting all believers, past, present and future, **free** from the penalty and bondage of sin, as a power and as a principle.

Jesus is now our lawyer, our advocate, before the Father. He intercedes with the Father continually on our behalf; He has never lost a "case." The Church, all believers, will spend eternity with Jesus Christ.

No one has ever seen the Father; Jesus made the Father known to His people. The world did not know or recognize Jesus; many did not receive Him.

Notes:

God, the Holy Spirit
Names of the Holy Spirit:

1 Breath of the Almighty Job 33:4
Life-giving breath of God.

2 Spirit of Counsel Isaiah 11:2
Counsels and teaches us.

3 Eternal Spirit Hebrew 9:14
"Eternal God"

4 Free Spirit Psalm 51:12
Generous and willing spirit.

5 God Acts 5:3-4
Third Member of the Godhead.

6 Good Spirit Nehemiah 9:20; Psalm 143:10
Teaches and leads us in all that is good.

7 Holy Spirit Psalm 51:11, Luke 11:13; Ephesians 1:13; 4:30
Spirit of holiness.

8 Power of the Highest Luke 1:35

9 Lord: 2 Corinthians 3:16-17

10 Counselor, Comforter John 14:16, 26; 15:26; Romans 8:26

The Holy Spirit is the third Person of the Trinity. He is equal to the Father and the Son and should be worshipped even as they are.

As a person, the Holy Spirit thinks, feels, purposes, knows, wills, loves and grieves.

The Holy Spirit also regenerates us and empowers us.

See Nehemiah 9:20; Romans 8:27; I Corinthians 2:10-12; Acts 1:8; Romans 15:30; Ephesians 4:30.

The Holy Spirit also searches the deeper things of God, can speak and cry out; He intercedes, teaches, testifies, leads and directs, commands, calls men to work and gives them tasks.

He proceeds on the mission to which He is sent. The Holy Spirit was assigned a definite office as our Comforter. He is a personal companion to every believer—our Comforter; Jesus sent Him to be by our side until we could once again be with Jesus Christ when He returns.

See I Corinthians 2:10; Revelations 2:7; Galatians 4:6; Romans 8:26; John 14:26; 15:26; Romans 8:14; Acts 16:6-7; 13:2; 20:28; John 14:6;15:26.

The Spirit gives power to overcome abnormal fear of the dark, insomnia, loneliness, a broken heart, helplessness. He guides in teaching, preaching and in talking to others about the Lord. We need to learn to communicate with him on a regular basis. The Spirit can best work in our lives when we give him the freedom to do so. He can fill you with a joy and contentment that no one can take away from you. Study your Bible and let Him teach you. You will discover new insights every time you read your way through God's holy Word.

I John 2:27 says, "But you have received the Holy Spirit, and he lives within you, so you don't need anyone to teach you what is true.

For the Spirit teaches you all things, and what he teaches is true - it is not a lie."

Summary

When you talk to God, you are actually talking to all three Persons of the Godhead, for they are **one** in unity. As Nicky Gumbel says, "We pray **to** the Father **through** Jesus Christ **by** the Holy Spirit."[3]

*The Godhead exists; God always existed,
exists now, and always will exist. God is eternal.*

That is a fact that our finite minds cannot fully understand; we have to believe that it is so or nothing in this world would make any sense at all.

In Hebrews 11:6b it says about God, "Anyone who wants to come to him must believe that there is a God and that he rewards those who sincerely seek him."

Romans 8:9-14 says, "But you are not controlled by your sinful nature. The Spirit controls you if you have the Spirit of God living in you. (And remember that those who do not have the Spirit of Christ living in them are not Christians at all.) Since Christ lives within you, even though your body will die because of sin, your spirit is alive because you have been made right with God. The Spirit of God, who raised Jesus from the dead, lives in you. And just as he raised Christ from the dead, he will give life to your mortal body by this same Spirit living within you.

"So, dear brothers and sisters, you have no obligation whatsoever to do what your sinful nature urges you to do. For if you keep on following your sinful nature, you will perish.

But if through the power of the Holy Spirit you turn from it and its evil deeds, you will live. For all who are led by the Spirit of God are children of God."

Notes:

Chapter Two

Chapter 2—Answering Major Questions

The Answer

I'm waiting for the answer, it surely must come soon
For God Himself has promised, my soul is all attune;
I've told Him all my failures, confessed my every si,
And now I walk with Jesus, His Spirit dwells within.

He told me I could trust Him, His Word I cannot doubt,
I know that He has heard me, He cannot cast me out;
I rest upon His promise, His own He'll not deny,
I'm waiting for the answer, the hour is drawing nigh.

This darkness soon must vanish, the day is now at hand,
I cannot see the future, and yet I firmly stand;
He promised to protect me, no matter what befall.
I know that He will help me, as on His name I call.

He saw me in my sorrow, He heard my feeble prayer,
I ventured all on Jesus, and cast on Him my care;
And now I have he answer, He did not say me nay,
Oh, may I magnify Him, and praise Him every day.

Hamilton, August 3l, 1946
From "Poems of a Lifetime by Dr. Oswald J. Smith

CHAPTER 2—Answering Some of the Major Questions

Why is God silent when we desperately need Him?

Why is it that God seems to ignore some of our prayers? Why do we not feel His presence at all times? There are important factors to take into consideration when considering the silence of God.

1 Sometimes God's silence is a result of deliberate sin caused by man's carelessness, neglect and folly. Galatians 6:7b reads in part, "You will always reap what you sow!"

God hears our prayers but He answers them in His own way and in His own timing. Sometimes his answer is not what we want. God acts and sees things on another level or on another plane or dimension.

Is it right that we should question the workings of the most holy God, our creator? In Isaiah 55:8, 9 we read, "My thoughts are completely different from yours," says the Lord. "And my ways are far beyond anything you could imagine."

We **can** learn to **trust God** even when we cannot possibly understand His reasons. God's plan for each one of us, along with the green pastures and quiet waters, includes sorrow, suffering and pain. It is through trials and difficulties that believers mature. These things are meant to build us up—not destroy us—by learning to put our faith and trust in God. He knows what is best for us in the bigger picture.

Talk to God; give Him your cares and concerns; leave your burdens and cares with Him; then step out in confidence. Trust God on the basis of His character.

2 Sin may be a reason for the situations we face, but it is not always the case! In John 9:3 we read about the man born blind, "It was not because of his sins or his parents' sins," Jesus answered. "He was born blind so the power of God could be seen in him."

In this case Jesus performed a miracle and healed his blindness. God had allowed this man to be born blind so that Jesus might be able to miraculously heal him. Why? So that the works of the Father might be displayed in him. Not having a right relationship with God is at best like not being "on the station" when you are trying to listen on your radio or TV, at worst it is like not having turned it on.

Gold ore is put through the refining fire several times before it becomes purified and useable in its most beautiful form.

Learning to handle trials and temptations is part of the purifying and refining process of maturing.

We will face these all our earthly life. God does not create the trials; but in His divine wisdom He does allow us to encounter them.

There may be many other reasons that God is silent; we might not know the answers now, but down the road God often reveals His reasons for the things He does.

Getting to Know God While He is Silent

It is in the silent times that we need to really press in to Him and trust Him to do what is right for us. When we obey what He has already said, He will show us more. This is a good time to build faith and trust in God. Love and worship Him; be faithful and obedient to His word.

Read your Bible; wait on Him in your quiet times. Give the Holy Spirit time to minister to you through God's Word. One powerful resource that we have, even during this time, is "praying in the spirit." Jude 20, 2l; Ephesians 6:18; Romans 8:27

God's silence does not last forever! We must learn to trust Him. Cling to God in faith and His presence will be made known to you. Even in the midst of fiery trials God is there, loving you and watching you. Tap into the strength God will give you during these times.

Meditate; imagine a picture of yourself with Jesus and His followers when He walked in Jerusalem, Nazareth and Galilee. Even before you "know" Him, God is working in your life to prepare you for when you will come to know Him. There are many situations where there are no easy answers.

"The spiritual life we need to develop goes beyond such questions, as pressing as they may seem. The basic point of spiritual awareness is to move from why? questions to yes! responses to God. We need to spend less time asking impossible questions and more time intensifying our relationship with the Father. Only by doing this can we become comfortable with mystery and learn to trust God's good providence to work out the tangles and discords of our lives."[1]

We have a tendency to forget God is beside us at all times, that He cares for us, and through faith we can see God anywhere.

When we forget, we begin to think of God as remote. We do things that we think He cannot see and think thoughts that He cannot know. Some even believe God doesn't exist at all, or if He does, that He doesn't care.

Hearing from God

Hearing from God is something we all want to learn more about, including me! I am not going to try to give an in-depth study on this subject, but I would like to share a few things that I have learned in this regard.

There are many good books available that give more teaching and information, which I do not need to repeat here.

God often uses visions and dreams as a means of speaking to us. Learning to interpret them can sometimes be a problem. Over the years God has given me spiritual dreams which have come to pass; on other occasions I have had dreams I could not interpret.

Sometimes you have to let them go; it is not always easy to decide which dreams are of God and which dreams are just normal dreaming. Sometimes our heart's desire can be so strong, that we dream about it—that does not make it a spiritual dream.

I have had a few visions that have already come to pass in great detail. One vision was a picture of my first husband, Gordon, lying in a copper coffin wearing a light blue suit. The background was a cream-colored cement block wall. At that time Gordon was very sick; God warned me with this vision that he was going to die. Six weeks later he died. When I bought the coffin, I did not remember the dream. I just bought the only one I could afford.,

When I went to view him at the funeral parlor, he was lying there in a light blue suit (the only one he owned) in a copper coffin (the only one I could afford to buy) and behind him was a cream-colored cement block wall! I had never seen the viewing room before.

So when I walked into that viewing room, I stopped dead in my tracks. For a minute I thought I was having my vision all over again. One difference...this time it was real. Visions are rare, but they are easier to recognize.

They usually come to you when you are awake; they are not dreams.

Now I would also like to share two dreams with you that also came to pass. I was desperately sick with SLE, an internal form of Lupus. For months I was constantly in and out of the hospital, being transported by ambulance back and forth between Three Hills and Calgary, AB. Medications had weakened my muscles so badly I couldn't even walk.

I was totally bedridden...and very discouraged.

Many people were praying for me, but nothing seemed to happen. Sound familiar?

Then I had two dreams in full color, several weeks apart. The second one was an explanation of the first one and added more. These dreams were very vivid; I can still see every detail of them to this day, several years later.

Dream One

I was on a holiday with my family high up in the mountains somewhere. We stopped at a small café for lunch. My brother-in-law, Henry, and I decided to walk out back and take a look at the scenery. We walked up to a railing that was on the edge of a very steep cliff and looked down into a deep gorge where a fast-moving river was roaring down the mountainside. There were jagged rocks and rapids all along it. It was an awesome and beautiful sight. Then it happened.

The railing I was leaning on broke, and I found myself falling over the side of the cliff! Henry grabbed for me but missed and almost fell himself. I felt like I was falling in slow motion; my mind was racing with all kinds of thoughts. I hollered goodbye to Henry and then looked down. It was a very long way, straight down. Strangely enough I felt no fear; I just wondered how it would feel when I landed in the river! It seemed to take forever! Yes, it's true. Your mind does speed up in desperate circumstances! All kinds of thoughts can quickly flow through your mind.

Just before I reached the river everything blanked out for a bit. When I came to, I was in the river that was flowing very swiftly and deep. It seemed like I was sitting in an invisible chair in the water with just my head and shoulders sticking out. The water felt warm and very soothing. I went flying past wicked boulders and around whirlpools, but not once did I hit a boulder or get sucked into a whirlpool. I was so amazed at this phenomenon that I forgot all about being afraid (Normally, I am afraid of being in deep water).

The scenery I passed was fascinating, tall jagged walls of a deep canyon with occasional little trees or shrubs hanging onto the sides of the cliffs. I just relaxed in my invisible chair and wondered what on earth was happening. Why didn't I feel anything when I hit the water? Why wasn't I dead? Maybe I was? I couldn't figure it out.

After what seemed a very long time the river opened out into a valley and started moving slow and easy. Suddenly, I felt sand under my feet! I had floated over into a quiet spot just a few feet from a sandy bank. I stood up and walked out onto the beach.

It was warm and pleasant there, so I just lay down on the sand to try to catch my breath and figure out what I was supposed to do next. I wasn't hurt anywhere, just very tired. I pinched myself; it hurt. I was definitely alive!

I finally sat up and looked around. There, way up the side of the hill was the highway! I decided to climb up the cliff and see if I could find my way back to the café from where it all began. I wondered if there would be police cars and an ambulance there and what everyone would think when I came wandering in amongst them wet and unhurt! It was a very long walk! I had evidently been carried very far downstream.

It took me a while, but I finally got there. Sure enough the police and an ambulance were there and men were down in the bottom of the canyon, by the river, looking for my body. My sudden appearance surprised everyone, but it was a time of great rejoicing and praising the Lord.

End of Dream One

I pondered over this dream for a long time, wondering just what it meant. I hoped it meant that the Lord was going to heal me soon; I clung to this hope. My husband, Peter and I, asked the Lord what it was all about, but no answer—at least not right away. The second dream I had when I was actually in the hospital; it was about two months later.

Dream Two

I was lying in my hospital bed when the door to my private room opened and a man walked in. He was carrying a brief case; I couldn't see his head and shoulders.

He started talking to me. He told me that God had decided it was time for me to know a bit of what was happening with regards to my illness! As you can imagine, I was all ears.

He opened his brief case and took out a large folded piece of paper and spread it out on a table next to my bed.

I leaned over to look at it. It was a diagram that showed the café where I had fallen and also the whole face of the cliff and the river that I had fallen into! I was totally amazed. I looked up into his face except that I still couldn't see it! I never did see his head and shoulders. I have often wondered if it was Jesus Himself or an angel. Someday I shall ask Him.

Pointing to the diagram, he started explaining it step by step. The broken rail and empty space was obvious. He said that Henry had almost fallen over the railing with me; that meant that he was very ill for a short while, but he recovered.

I thought back to when I had the first dream; Henry had been in the hospital at the same time I was with heart problems! And he had recovered and gone home! I began to feel excited; what did my falling into the river mean?

The messenger told me that my fall towards the river was the long period of weeks that I would be seriously ill, and I was, six months of illness! I was still in the hospital.

Then he answered another of my questions. Why did I black out and then find myself in the river? He said that God had sent an angel to catch me and place me gently in the river so that I wouldn't die! Why was the water warm? God was in the process of healing me in that river! Then the most interesting part yet was next.

He said I was already through falling down the cliff and that I was currently in the river, that I would be in the river for a long period of time. When I climbed out onto the beach, I knew I would be well again. No time period was given.

End of Dream Two

What happened after that? About two weeks later I started walking again a little bit; I was able to get around in a wheel chair, then later a walker, then a cane, then I could walk by myself. This process took several weeks, but I was elated. I spent two years on a regimen of cyclophosphamide, and then I was completely well from the SLE! It was a long time, just as he had promised in the dream.

Everything was planned and orchestrated by a wonderful God. He does things His own way. He could have healed me instantly, but He chose, for His own reasons, to use medical doctors, who were guided through the combined prayers of the saints, to heal me!

I am still in the process of healing from the damage caused by all the medications that I had consumed.

I wouldn't trade those three or four years for anything because through it all I was able to get to know my Lord better and began to heal from all my spiritual hurts and wounds from my past. I just hope and pray that my sharing this bit of my testimony with you will help you to understand what spiritual dreams can be and how they differ from visions.

Satan can also put dreams into our heads; these are usually fairly easy to recognize. If you feel that you have had a spiritual dream, either from God or from the enemy, you need to check it out against the Word of God.

If it deviates in any way from the principles and teachings in the Bible, it is not of God. Talk to God about it and in a conscious deliberate act renounce and reject it in the name of Jesus Christ.

Another thing you need to do. Test your own inner feelings about what the dream is showing you. If it is something you don't want to do or feel to be wrong, don't act upon it until you know that it is true to scripture and comes from God. Check it out thoroughly.

Fact: God's voice will sound like your own voice and
Satan's voice will also sound like your own voice.
Frustrating!

However, a dream that is truly from God will always follow the principles and teachings in the Bible. If you cannot discern whether your dream is from God or not, I would advise you to get counsel from your pastor or another believer you know and trust before making any decisions based on what you saw in your dream. Whatever you do, do not make hasty decisions based on a dream or vision until you know beyond a shadow of a doubt that it is from God.

Even a prophetic dream that is a message from God often needs to be nurtured by prayer and seeking God before it comes to pass. In Psalm 119:49 we read, "Remember your promise to me, for it is my only hope." In Nehemiah 1:8 we read, "Please remember what you told your servant Moses…"

We need to keep reminding the Lord of His word and His promises, believing He will do as He promised.

As you mature in your Christian walk, you will gradually learn to discern what is of God and what is not. Sometimes you may make a mistake or a misjudgment. Do not be alarmed. God knows we are human and that we are striving to learn how to hear from Him.

Ask Him for forgiveness and keep striving to know God better. Ask the Holy Spirit to guide and teach you.

How many times will God forgive us? EVERY time we sincerely ask Him. You have to mean it, not just say…now I can go out and sin some more. That is not true repentance! God knows our weaknesses and will strengthen us as we seek His help.

Sometimes the best thing to do is to write the dream or vision in a journal and set it aside and just wait to see what evolves. If it is prophetic and it comes to pass, you will know that it was from God.

It is so easy to give God credit for our dreams and then when they don't come to pass, we get angry with God; they probably were not from God at all! Remember that **Satan can give you dreams in an effort to turn you away from God.**

As you study the Word of God and pray on a daily basis, your ability to hear from God will improve. The closer your relationship with Him, the better you will know His heart. I am still striving to reach this goal myself. I long to know God better; I desire to hear Him when He speaks to me!

Ask God to give you a real hunger to be able to communicate with Him. Building a relationship with God is the prime key. The closer our relationship with God, the easier it is to hear from Him and know His will for our lives. Trust God; He will never let you down. Sometimes it will feel like He has. This is when you have to TRUST HIM the most. Review the principles I shared about the silence of God.

Should God always rescue us?

God does not always rescue us, in terms of this life. Things are not always as they appear; we live, as it were, in two dimensions, the world that we can see with our natural eyes and the spiritual world that is unseen but very real. **Sometimes He uses us for His glory from within our situation.**

Life always comes out of a "death" experience. God has the "after" in mind.

Sometimes the "after" is only realized when we leave this life to spend eternity with God.

In I Peter 1:6-7 we read, "So be truly glad! There is wonderful joy ahead, even though it is necessary for you to endure many trials for a while.

It is being tested as fire tests.

If your faith remains strong after being tried by fiery trials, it will bring you much praise and glory and honor on the day when Jesus Christ is revealed to the whole world.

Only those who have passed through suffering and sorrow can effectively comfort others. Learn to think positively and live according to the knowledge that you have, but constantly strive to learn more.

If you trust Him during the valley experiences, you can have peace in your soul, for **God cares about you!** In John 13:7 Jesus tells Peter, "You don't understand now why I am doing it; someday you will." **Embrace God during the silent times!**

No enemy can come so near that God is not nearer.

What is sin?

The dictionary calls sin "transgression, evil, a violation of an accepted moral, religious or social code."

In God's eyes sin is **any** lack of conformity to the character of God, **whether an act or state**. Sin is a condition, a state of being. Sin, as an act or as a state of being, cannot be hidden, Numbers 32:23; Proverbs 28:13.

God sees and uncovers hidden acts of sins. Remember that God is everywhere! The result of sin is death. We commit sins, by acts or deeds. Sin is also **a state of being**. We are born into the human race, which has inherited a sinful nature. We ALL have to repent of our sins before God can commune with us.

There is **no one** that is good, not even one! No matter how good you are, you are still a sinner and need the salvation provided by Jesus Christ.

Sin involves our refusal to respond to God's word and to enter the relationship for which we were created.

We seek to find within ourselves the justification for our existence. We seek to find the meaning of our destiny merely in our relationship with the created world in the context of our immediate environment. (You might want to listen to the song called "The Well" by Casting Crowns on YouTube.)

The result is that our life has often been characterized by bondage, conflict with evil powers, frailty and frustration. We can be so perverted and evil in our minds and hearts that we turn the truth of God into a lie; we become the followers of Satan.

See Romans 10:3; Romans 1:25; Hebrews 2:14:15; Ephesians 6:12; Isaiah 40:6; Job 14:1; Genesis 8:2; Job 14:4; Psalm 51:5; Matthew 12:39; 15:19-20; Romans 1:25

Either you follow Jesus Christ or you follow Satan;
there is no right way to do a wrong thing.
There is no other choice, no middle ground.

Notes:

Why did God allow Sin and Evil to enter a perfect world?

There is a definite distinction between the **active** will of God and His **permissive** will. The entrance of sin into the world must be attributed to the permissive will of God, since sin is a contradiction of His holiness. There is an area in which God's **will** to act is dominant and there is an area in which man's **liberty** is given permission to act.

The Bible shows both in action. God brings nation against nation **because they do not serve and obey His will**. In Matthew 24:6-8 Jesus says that there will always be wars and rumors of wars. Nation will rise against nation, kingdom against kingdom, and in various places there will be famines and earthquakes. Jesus said these things must take place.

I know of no way to explain any of this; it is a mystery known only to God. God says the above is so, and there is nothing we can do but trust Him.

As is true in all wars, there are the innocent ones who suffer. All down through Biblical history into our present times innocent individuals have been caught up in God's judgment. Through most of this life we suffer because of sin, our own or of others, especially of evil men and their agendas motivated by the devil.

There is one consolation. When believers die, they go instantly to be with Jesus. Believers who do not die but suffer terribly because of these wars are not forgotten. God sees them and is with them at all times. God knows the plans He has for each believer, and we have to learn to trust Him in this, no matter how terrible it is. He knows and understands our feelings and our needs.

It is like a little bird sitting on a tree limb singing his heart out while in the midst of a terrible storm. We need to be like that little bird, praising and worshipping God in the midst of our trials and temptations. Our rewards will be eternal even if there are none on earth. There is a reason for everything, but we may never know what those reasons are until we meet with Jesus in heaven.

God's will is often a mystery, because we do not see the full picture. God gives us grace for tomorrow when we need it, not before. All we have to do is keep pressing in to Him and commune with Him. We will have grace for tomorrow when tomorrow gets here.

God created mankind with a will; this enabled him to make choices. God did not want puppets or robots serving Him.

God wanted a people who would choose to love Him and obey him because they wanted to do so.

The forbidden tree in the middle of the garden was put there on purpose, so that Adam and Eve would have to exercise their will and choose for themselves whom they would serve.

They failed miserably. God knew they would fail, so He had already planned a way to rescue them, so that they would have another chance to choose Him and become acceptable to a holy and just God.

The answer was Jesus Christ who would come to be the Redeemer of mankind more than 4000 years later.

Jesus gave up his life for us by death on the cross; while on the cross He took upon himself all the sins of the world—past, present and future. Now we can be righteous in the Father's eyes as he looks at us through the sacrifice made by Him and His Son for our benefit.

Romans 5:1-5 reads as follows: "By faith we have been made acceptable to God. And now, because of our Lord Jesus Christ, we live at peace with God. Christ has also introduced us to God's underserved kindness on which we take our stand. So we are happy, as we look forward to sharing in the glory of God. But that's not all! We gladly suffer, because we know that suffering helps us to endure. And endurance builds character, which gives us a hope that will never disappoint us. All of this happens because God has given us the Holy Spirit, who fills our heart with his love."

Sin will take you farther than you want to go,
keep you longer than you want to stay,
cost you more than you want to pay.

Notes:

Chapter Three

And God spoke...

*All that I have seen teaches me
to trust the Creator
for all that I have not seen.*

CHAPTER 3—"In the Beginning God..."

*Genesis shows the path from the human perspective
of how you come
into relationship with the God of heaven.*

God is eternal; He always was, is and He always will be, see John 1.1. Before the world and the heavens were created time as we know it did not exist. Time came into existence when God created the world. Time will once again cease to exist when Jesus Christ returns for all the believers and our **current world** is destroyed.

God will create a new heaven and a **new earth** for the redeemed believers, but it will be without time; it will be for eternity.

The Bible does not explain nor describe the creation event; it only declares that it was achieved by the will of God.

How did the world begin?

"The author of the Creation Story, Moses, lived thousands of years ago. Yet, consider what he declared:

- ✓ The universe had a beginning.
- ✓ Time had a beginning.
- ✓ The young Earth was desolate and void of life.
- ✓ The surface of the earth was blanketed in darkness.
- ✓ The earth was covered by water.
- ✓ Light finally illuminated the surface of the earth.

*The scientific validity of all of these
statements has been confirmed.*

If we were to disregard divine inspiration, we could not begin to explain how an author living so long ago could have acquired such knowledge."[4]

Pre Creation Period

Space, time, matter and light (energy) did not exist, as we know it. God was and is complete in Himself; He is spirit; His existence is independent of time and space. God's creating the universe was not an extension of Himself; what He created was not divine.

He did not **need** a universe or human beings. However, He created a Master Plan; He **wanted** to create a universe, an earth and a people who would love Him, worship and honor Him—a people with whom He could commune and fellowship. He did not want robots; He could have created them by the millions, but that is not what He wanted.

"...God created the heavens and the earth."

Note: God tells us a little bit about how He did all this creation, but God does not give us the scientific details; He just wants us to know what He has done.

Refuting Revolution

At this point I am going to address the argument given by evolutionists that the world happened by chance, natural selection, over millions of years! It actually takes more "faith" to believe the doctrine of evolution, then it does to have "faith" that an Intelligent Mind, God, is the one behind ALL creation.

Are Darwin and his followers responsible? If Darwin is right, we are just sophisticated monkeys! This would mean that the Bible is wrong, that there is no right or wrong. We can just make up our morals and laws as we go. Belief in his theory attempts to destroy all we believe from the Bible. That is why our world is sliding down a long, slippery slope towards destruction!

[22]As Oxford evolutionist Dawkins said: "The more you understand the significance of evolution, the more you are pushed away from an agnostic position and towards atheism."

Agnostics believe that it is impossible to have any knowledge of God. Atheists believe there is no God.

[19]"It has been said that you can have God or natural selection, but you cannot have both.

"Science teaches us many true things, and some of those things point toward God...scientific evidence actually supports theistic belief.

In fact, across a wide range of sciences, evidence has come to light in the last fifty years which, taken together, provides a robust case for theism. Only theism can provide an intellectually satisfying causal explanation for all of this evidence."[19]

[20]"If modern cosmologists agree that the universe had a beginning, then this implies a cause that transcends the universe. Whatever begins to exist has a cause. The universe began to exist. Therefore, the universe has a cause."

[21]"But now, modern astrophysics and astronomy have dropped into the lap of Christians precisely that, according to Aquinas, makes God's existence virtually undeniable. Given that whatever begins to exist has a cause and that the universe began to exist, there must be some sort of transcendent cause for the origin of the universe.

"Contemporary scientists are discovering that the laws of physics are fine-tuned to permit life. Biology shows that there is a lot of information in the cells that also suggests intelligent design."

[19]"To get life going in the first place would have required biological information; the implications point beyond the material realm to a prior intelligent cause. **Science.**"

Creation Week
Day One

[5]"On the first day of creation **God spoke into existence** (emphasis is mine) space, time, matter and then light, i.e. energy…Space, time and matter were brought into existence as amorphous raw materials out of which God would make the universe and finally the earth."

During creation week the usual laws of physics were not in effect. We should not attempt to understand creation week by extrapolating from present day laws and facts to arrive at our conclusions.

God created the **entire** heavens and earth at the beginning of the first day. This included the sun, moon and stars. The light came from the sun shining on an orbiting earth! I will discuss this more on Day Four.

God now concentrated on our earth. The Spirit of God hovered or brooded over its surface. The Holy Spirit was bringing forth life in fulfillment of God's spoken command.

God spoke and the Holy Spirit did the work. One of the Psalmists likens creation to a birthing. We are told that the earth was formless and void, covered with water and that it was enveloped in darkness.

Then God spoke and created light.

[6]"There are photons of all wavelengths in the universe. Light is a form of energy. God himself is light. However, God is infinitely more than energy. God called the light 'day' and he called the dark 'night.' The fact that there was day and night tells us that the light shining on the earth was directional (from one source)."

This completed the first day of creation and God saw that it was good.

Day Two

[4]"The sun is the catalyst of the hydrologic cycle, and light was finally visible on the surface of the earth when Day Two began.

"God separated the waters, creating a space of 40,000 to 70,000 feet in height, possibly more. God called this expanse 'sky.' Water now existed in both its liquid and gaseous states. Science tells us that a stable water cycle began at that time."

How did He do it? Perhaps He created tremendous heat and the waters rose from the surface of the water in the form of steam until it settled above and around the earth where God wanted it placed.

It is generally believed that the water above the sky was probably in the form of a very heavy mist and thick enough to protect earth from harmful rays coming from space. The actual amount of sunlight that filtered through the mist at this point is anyone's guess. This most likely produced a greenhouse effect all over the earth.

Day Three

On the third day God said, "Let the waters beneath the sky be gathered into one place so dry ground may appear." And so it was. God named the dry ground "land" and the water "seas."

[4]"It was around this time that tectonic plates began to form. The cornerstones of the continents began to emerge out of the water.

While the seafloor mostly consists of dark, heavy, basaltic rock, the land is composed of lighter, granitic rock called a 'craton,' which tends to rise above sea level like an object floating on water."

These cratons were thrust violently upward and moved quickly and freely above the earth's watery surface. These moving cratons collided, merged, and formed large landmasses.

Eventually, the earth stopped this vertical movement. It was then that the sliding process we understand as plate tectonics truly began, and the continents began to form. All this took place on day three.

The above information is not meant to be a scientific explanation, but attempts to explain just a little of what actually happened to the earth when God spoke and the land appeared on the surface of the earth. God saw that it was good.

"Then God said, 'Let the **land** burst forth with every sort of grass and seed-bearing plant. And let there be trees that grow seed-bearing fruit. The seeds will then produce the kinds of plants and trees from which they came.' And so it was." Genesis 1:11

This activity included the earth under the water as well as the earth above the water. God did not state that only the dry land was to grow vegetation, but the whole earth – all the **land**, wet and dry. Science has proven this to be a fact. Vegetation in the seas came before any life forms were created.

[4]"In the seas and on the land, science has established that plants preceded animals."

At this time God had not yet sent rain upon the earth and there was no one there to cultivate the soil. Instead, a mist used to rise from the earth and water the whole surface of the ground. See Genesis 2:1-6.

More and more plants took root and began to grow. They multiplied throughout the earth, each reproducing their own seed. The grasses became long and lush, the fruit trees and seed-bearing plants were growing all over the face of the earth. The seas were filled with all kinds of growing plants as well.

God had a Master Plan! God's basic greenhouse was now ready for the rest of his creation work. This completed the third day of God's creation and God saw that it was good.

Day Four

On the fourth day that "God said, 'I command lights to appear in the sky and to separate day from night and to show the time for seasons, special days, and years. I command them to shine on the earth.' And that is what happened.

"God made two powerful lights, the brighter one to rule the day and the other to rule the night. He also made the stars.

Then God put these lights in the sky to shine on the earth, to rule by day and night, to separate light from darkness.

"God looked at what He had done, and it was Good. Evening came and then morning—that was the fourth day." . Genesis 1:14-19

This was necessary to support the various life forms He was about to create upon the earth on days 5 and 6.

Day Five

"And God said, 'Let the waters swarm with fish and other life. Let the skies be filled with birds of every kind.' So God created great sea creatures and every sort of fish and every kind of bird. And God saw that it was good." Genesis 1:20:21

God blessed His creations and told them to be fruitful and to multiply on the earth. All the necessary food supply for the various forms of life created this day was waiting for them. Some believe that dinosaurs and all the related creatures of this kind were created on this day. Others believe they were created at the beginning of the sixth day. It is possible that all the insects and bugs were also created on this day. Again, they are not mentioned specifically in the Biblical account, but we know they are here!

Birds were not the only flying creatures created during this day. The Hebrew word does not make such a distinction. Any creature capable of flight would be included. Amphibians were probably included in this day's creation. Some of God's creatures were created to start life in the seas and continue life on land. God planned it all!

Point of interest!

God commanded his creatures to multiply and fill the seas by reproducing.

Such a command implies a great surge in the diversity and multitude of life in the seas.

Science agrees with this order of things!

Non-creationist scientists claim that millions of years ago there was a sudden and prodigious explosion of diverse marine life that science has named the Cambrian Explosion. They claim that over a period of ten million years every animal phyla that exists today **abruptly appeared** in the earth's water.[4,6] Of course they have the number of years incorrect according to God's Word, but they do acknowledge that the surge of life in the seas all happened at once!

Science has no real explanation for this. Creationists do. They were spoken into existence by a Divine Being, God. Regardless of the creation theory to which you hold, this discovery by the scientists bears witness to the fact that life in the seas was fast and "explosive."

This part fits all the creation theories very well. The Bible does not detail all forms that God created—only the ones that would directly play a part in the lives of the people He was about to create. God was very busy this day.

He must have a wonderful sense of humor; take a close look at some of the sea creatures and birds and myriads of insects that He created! This completed the fifth day of creation and God saw that it was good.

Day Six

The sixth day was God's final day for creating and the climax to all that he was doing. By this time the earth was a very lush green planet with no deserts anywhere. God had to provide natural lawn mowers to cut the grasses so that others could walk about on it. The vegetation was probably like a tropical jungle, also needing large animals to keep it in control.

On this day in their proper order God made all sorts of wild animals, livestock and small animals, each able to reproduce its own kind. The giant dinosaurs and all their type would have made wonderful lawnmowers! All the other wild animals, both large and small would have followed these; they were followed by all sorts of livestock. God instructed them to multiply and fill the whole earth. They did.

Now God began his final and crowning act of creation; He spent the rest of this day creating a man in his own image—patterned after Himself.

Now the earth was ready for that which it had been so carefully prepared! God made a beautiful garden on the earth that he called Eden.

In this garden God planted every tree that was pleasing to the sight and good for food; the tree of life and the tree of the knowledge of good and evil were in the middle of the garden. God then placed Adam in the garden He had prepared for him. God told Adam he could eat from every tree in the garden except of the tree of the knowledge of good and evil. If he ate from that tree, in "that day" he would die.

A river flowed out of Eden to water the garden; from there it divided and became four rivers. Pishon River surrounded the whole land of Havilah, where there were rich deposits of gold. Aromatic resin and onyx stones were also found there.

The Gihon River flowed around the entire land of Cush. The Tigris River flows to the east of Asshur, and the fourth river is the Euphrates.

During the universal flood over 1600 years later, many landscapes were changed. As a result no one knows exactly where Eden was or the exact course of the rivers before the flood. People have been hunting for years; the possible riches alone drawing some, religious desires driving others. The garden was either destroyed in the flood (or permanently hidden at this time), when everything else, except Noah and his family perished. The seeds in the earth did not die, for once the land started drying out, plant life started springing up all over the earth.

Adam's first task was to name all the animals. God brought them before Adam one by one "to see what he would call them." Whatever he called them that became their name.

Adam must have had a magnificent mind to accomplish such a feat. I cannot begin to comprehend how he could come up with so many names and remember them. Adam was created the way God meant all humans to be!

Not one of all the creatures was a suitable companion for Adam, so God caused a deep sleep to fall upon Adam. While he was asleep, God took one of his ribs and created Eve, the first woman. In Genesis 2:21 it says, "So the Lord God caused Adam to fall into a deep sleep. He took one of Adam's ribs and closed up the place from which he had taken it.

Then the Lord made a woman from the rib and brought her to Adam." In Genesis 2:23 Adam exclaimed, "At last!...she is part of my own flesh and bone!

She will be called 'woman' because she was taken out of a man."

From that point onward all descendants were born through the woman. Only Eve came from the bone of her husband.

God blessed Adam and Eve and He gave them the creation mandate: Multiply upon the earth. God also gave them dominion over all that He had created. They were to cultivate and take care of the garden.

This completed the sixth day of creation and God saw that it was good.

Summary of Day Six
- God created every kind of animal—wildlife, large and small, and livestock.
- God created Adam and placed him in the garden.
- God brought all the animals and birds to Adam so that he could give them a name.
- God fashioned a mate for Adam out of his own rib. He called her "woman" because she had been fashioned from his own rib.
- God blessed them and told them to multiply upon the earth.
- They were to care for the garden and take dominion over all the earth, including all the living creatures that God had created.

At this time Adam and Eve were naked, but neither of them felt any shame. That was the way God had made them and they were content. God also told them that the seed-bearing plants and all the fruit trees were for their food.

The grasses and other green plants were to be food for the birds and animals.

Point of Interest
[4]"Science and the Bible are in agreement on one fundamental aspect of man's creation. Modern man made a very late appearance on planet Earth.

This Biblical fact should not be minimized. This is the one claim that the Bible made about man's creation that can be scientifically verified—and it has been confirmed. The Bible may not be very specific or explanatory in its scientific statements. It may not satisfy the demands of science in its explanation, its reasoning, or its methodology. This is because the Bible's primary objective is to reveal God's message to humanity, and not to answer the riddles of science."

Day Seven

God rested from His work of creation. God's resting did not mean He was tired and now needed to rest, but rather it meant that He ceased to work. His acts of creation were completed. Now God could enjoy the people He had created. In the cool of the evenings the Lord God would walk with them in the garden and commune with them.

Throughout the Creation story the theme is indisputable. "Every natural process, every natural system, every law of science, and all life, matter, and energy that exists within our universe today are derived from one, omnipotent source, and that is the Hebrew God of the Holy Bible. Not even modern science has been able to repudiate this scientific statement, which is the very foundation of the Biblical Creation."[4]

God didn't care about the timeline, so why should we? God just wanted us to know what He had done!

The only real difference between the various theories 'out there' is the time involved for the actual creation to take place. Scientists agree to the order of the creation, but some still believe it was evolution and not creation.

God still created everything from nothing, regardless of the time theory you personally choose to believe. Evolution is not an option! Since none of us were there to give testimony, there is no way to prove any one particular theory beyond a shadow of a doubt; I am not even going to try to do so. We have to accept God's testimony; He is the only One who was actually there!

What is interesting, many non-believing scientists and evolutionists have come to a strong conclusion that the beginning of life and creation had to have been accomplished by an intelligent mind!

That is a big step for them to take. Of course Christians believe this based on what we read in God's Word. However, evolutionists and atheists do not generally agree with this. But as science discovers more and more amazing things, it proves more and more that an intelligent mind is behind everything.

Atheists and agnostics do not want to believe this because they do not want to be accountable to God for what they do with their lives! It is much more pleasant to believe in evolution which allows them what they consider total freedom to do as they wish.

In actuality they are following a god, Satan, and are doing exactly what he wants them to do!

Even though evolutionists cannot explain how life began, they have all kinds of theories of how things slowly over millions of years came together from nothing to begin life! They can fool people easily because of their knowledge and so many people believe what others tell them without investigating for themselves. That is just the way it is!

All evolutionists' suppositions, one-by-one, have been proven false! They still cannot explain how a single living cell came into being in the first place.

They talk only about fossils and millions of years, none of which can be proven by science.

Over the last fifty years Cosmetology, Biology, Archeology, Physics and Quantum Theories are all showing very strong evidence that there had to be an intelligent mind that started everything and then orchestrated all the necessary ingredients needed for life to come together at the right time and in the right way.

If you put all the materials needed into a room and sealed it tight and came back in millions of years, it would still be just a room filled with materials. The materials have to come together in very specific ways for life to evolve!

*It takes more faith to believe in evolution
then it does to believe in Biblical creation!*

NOTE: if you want the facts I refer to above in full detail and with scientific explanations, read Lee Strobel's book, "The Case for Creation." Excellent and informative reading.

God has a Master Plan for the earth and for the people that He has placed upon the earth. That is what matters to God!

The events in Genesis 1 and 2 were not meant to be scientific records but historical records of events that happened. If God wanted to give us a scientific record He could have done so. God preferred to have us trust Him to believe what He tells us is true. God just wanted us to understand our beginnings and the fact that mankind is indeed unique—made in the image of God! God is concerned with relationships, not education.

For what purpose did God create man?

In Genesis 1:27 we read that people were created "in the image of God." Our responsibility is towards our Creator. Only in this response can we be what we truly are meant to be. God involves Himself in a closer relationship with us than with all the rest of His creations.

In Matthew 4:4 we read, "People need more than bread for their life; they must feed on every word of God." God's Word, by which people live, offers them a relationship that lifts them above the rest of creation around them, and confers on them their dignity as a child of God, made in God's image and reflecting His glory.

It is as people are relating within their family and social relationships that they truly reflect the image of God. See Genesis 1:27-28 and 2:18.

The Creator knows you well;
do you know him at all?

What did God create when He created man in God's image?

God created man as a tripartite being; man consists of three component parts; body, soul and spirit. See I Thessalonians 5:23. The distinctions between the soul and spirit are not always clear, but they do exist. Let's take a closer look at these three components, body, soul and spirit.

The Body—World-consciousness

The body of man has five senses: sight, hearing, taste, touch and smell. The body was created from the dust and the earth and, once death takes over, returns to the dust from whence it came. Dust is analyzed as containing 96 elements; the body of man also contains 96 elements; they are identically the same.

Point of Interest
According to scientists' studying the human anatomy the human body contains one thousand miles (2,413,500 kms) of blood vessels, one million, five hundred thousand sweat glands, and that the lungs are composed of seven hundred million cells?

We have three trillion nerve cells of which nine billion are in the cerebral cortex of the brain!

Our veins are balanced with thirty million white and thirty thousand trillion red corpuscles!

We read in Psalm 139:14, "Thank you for making me so wonderfully complex! Your workmanship is marvelous - and how well I know it."

The Soul—Self-consciousness
The soul provides man with the ability to be a person and have a personality. It stands for the individual, personal life. The soul is the organ of our body that contains our mind and emotions and our will, our ability to make choices.

The soul seems to be the part of man midway between the body and the spirit, yet it is not a mixture of the two. The soul joins two worlds, the physical and the spiritual. The soul was actually created when the spirit, the breath of life, entered the body. The soul coordinates the activities of the body and the spirit. The soul must keep the body in subjection to the spirit, as the spirit is the part of man that communicates with God e.g. the soul is our computer that connects our spirit to God.

The Spirit—God-consciousness
This provides man with the ability to communicate with God. Man was made for God; He desires fellowship with man. See Genesis 3:8; Hebrews 10:39; James 1:21; Psalm 49:8 God breathed (wind, breath) into the nostrils of Adam, giving him the spirit. The spirit receives impressions of outward and material things through the soul and the body, but it belongs to a higher level, a higher dimension, and is capable of a direct knowledge of God by its own higher senses and faculties.

God is spirit - John 4:24. The spirit of man is the part that resembles God most, Romans 8:16; Ecclesiastes 12:7; 3:21.

At death the soul/spirit of the believer goes upward to God; the soul/spirit of the unbeliever goes downward to Satan and hell, Luke 16:22-26.

Up to the time of Christ's resurrection the spirit and soul of the believer at death went to paradise, a place especially prepared for believers inside the earth. A great gulf separated paradise from hell. Read the story of the

rich man who died and went to hell in Luke 16:19-31, which was just across a great gulf from paradise, for confirmation of this fact.

After Christ's resurrection the believers were removed from paradise and went to be with Him in heaven where Jesus now reigns with the Father. In the final great resurrection the body, the soul and the spirit of believers will once again be reunited. Our new bodies will be incorruptible. Revelations 21:4-8.

The tree of life will once again be available to all believers. Revelations 22:14.

Notes:

The Fall of Man

At the time when God placed Adam in the garden, he was told that he could eat of all the trees in the garden except of the one in the middle of the garden, the tree of the knowledge of good and evil. He was told that if he ate of that tree he would surely die that day.

God fashioned Eve after Adam was in the garden. It was his responsibility to tell Eve about the tree. Apparently he had; she knew about it when she was talking to the serpent.

In order to have man worship Him of his own free will, he had to be able to have a choice to obey Him or not obey Him. The ability to choose for himself whom he would like to serve gave him a free will.

Adam and Eve probably did not really understand what God meant by death, for they had never seen death. However, they did know beyond a doubt that God had forbidden them to eat of that particular tree and knew severe judgment would come upon them if they chose to do so.

However, day after day they would look at that tree and wonder just what the fruit would taste like. In Genesis 3:6 it says that the fruit looked fresh and delicious. Plus, eating the fruit would make them wise! The temptation to taste it and become wise must have been very strong.

One day when Adam and Eve were in the garden together, they walked over and looked at the tree. The serpent was there also, by the tree.

There an ancient book I discovered in a large college library claiming that the serpent was a very beautiful creature, that he had wings and could fly. They also said that the serpent was a best friend of Eve and that he use to fly her around Eden on his back! They enjoyed conversations together. Therefore, she was ready to be deceived by this serpent. This could be the very reason Satan chose the serpent to deceive Eve.

This is very possible when you consider the rest of the story. The serpent had allowed Satan to enter into him. This was soon to become his own undoing. Satan, through the serpent, spoke to Eve and tempted her to take and eat the fruit, telling her that she would not die. Instead, she would become wise like God, knowing good and evil. The idea of becoming wise appealed to her and the fruit did look good to eat.

She just had to taste it and see what would happen. She took one and ate it and then gave a fruit to Adam, too, and he ate it. He didn't even try to warn her or stop her! He was right there with her and let her eat the fruit.

That is part of what made his sin worse then the sin of Eve. She was deceived; Adam wasn't. He did it knowing He was disobeying God. Perhaps he was afraid he would lose Eve if he didn't eat the fruit, too…maybe someday we will know. What we do know for sure is that he ate the fruit in the full knowledge that he was disobeying God.

When he did so, both their eyes were instantly opened, and they knew good and evil, just as the serpent had stated. However, from that point on they physically began to die but spiritual death was immediate—separation from God. That was the real lie of Satan that they would not die. **Sin** entered the world by this one act of disobedience on their part. They were instantly separated from the Father by this act, as the Father's holiness could not tolerate disobedience.

God's judgment was instant and severe. He killed an animal and clothed their nakedness with animal skins. He sent them both out of the garden forever and placed the cherubim, and the flaming sword that turned in every direction, at the entrance of the garden to keep them away from the tree of life that would have allowed them to live forever. They were condemned to die.

When Adam and Eve were exiled from Eden, they had to cultivate their own garden. **God cursed the ground because of their disobedience**; the garden grew many weeds, so now they had to till the soil by the sweat of their brows to produce a crop. Before this time the garden grew unhindered by weeds.

Eve was promised **more** intense pain in child bearing as part of her punishment. Both Adam and Eve were now spiritually dead, but they were physically alive and toiled for many years. They had many sons and daughters.

The serpent was cursed for allowing Satan to use him in deceiving Eve and was told that he would forevermore go about on his belly eating the dust of the earth, implying that his method of movement had been something different up to this point—legs or perhaps wings? Maybe someday we will know.

He was also told that from now on he and the woman would be enemies; his offspring and her offspring would be enemies.

Women do hate snakes, right? Satan was told that he would strike the heel of her offspring, but that her offspring would crush his head. This was a prophecy of the crucifixion and resurrection of Jesus thousands of years later. It has since been fulfilled.

Satan has been permitted to stay on earth for a set period of time, but in the end God will cast Satan and his demons into the lake of fire that never diminishes. Hell was not created for people; God created hell for Satan and his angels. It is a sad fact that many people choose to join him instead of following and believing in God.

However, men and women who **choose** to follow Satan will in the end find themselves in hell **with** Satan and his angels.

This grieves God greatly, but He gave us a free will, knowing that some of the human race would turn their backs on Him. The Holy Spirit is constantly wooing people to come back to God, **but God will never force anyone to love and worship him**.

EVERY child of God has
a special place in God's plan.

Who is Lucifer?

When Satan was in heaven, his name was Lucifer. Now he is most commonly known as Satan or the Devil, the name of the prince of evil. His name basically means "adversary."

Where did he come from and who is he? Lucifer is a created being, so are all the angels.

The Apostle Paul stated that it is Christ through whom God created everything in heaven and earth. He made the things we can see, as well as all the things we cannot see—kings, kingdoms, rulers, and authorities. Everything was created through Him and for Him. He existed before everything else began and holds all creation together. See Colossians 2:16-17.

From the words of Ezekiel we have a description of Lucifer in a message from God: "You were the perfection of wisdom and beauty.

You were in Eden, the garden of God.

"Your clothing was adorned with every precious stone—red carnelian, chrysolite, white moonstone, beryl, onyx, jasper, sapphire, turquoise, and emerald—all beautifully crafted for you and set in the finest gold. They were given to you on the day you were created. I ordained and anointed you as the mighty angelic guardian.

"You had access to the holy mountain of God and walked among the stones of fire. You were blameless in all you did from the day you were created **until the day evil was found in you**." Ezekiel 28:12b-15

Satan's ultimate defeat and destruction was prophesied years before it happened. The death and resurrection of Jesus Christ defeated Satan. His final destruction will take place at the end of the age when believers will go to be with the Lord for eternity. Unbelievers and Satan, along with all his angels, will be cast into the lake of eternal fire.

Lucifer and his angels were cast out of heaven. It is now Satan's desire to control the earth; he wants all human beings to worship him! He even tried to get Jesus to worship him when He was in the desert after His water baptism.

When Adam and Eve sinned, Adam gave away his dominion or authority over the world. By His death on the cross and His resurrection, Jesus took back that authority from Satan. Now a "man," Jesus, once again has authority over the earth; Jesus is the second Adam. He has authority for all eternity. Satan was defeated and cast down.

Satan already knows the world will never be his to rule. He is doing everything he can prevent Jesus Christ from ruling the world; if he can't have it himself, then nobody else will, in his mindset, especially Jesus Christ and His followers. Satan is responsible for the terrible condition of the earth. If you want to blame someone, blame Satan, not God!

Do you have something against God?

Take a look at what God has against us! We have abused Him in every way possible; we have turned our backs on Him; we have blamed Him for all our troubles, for the current state of the world. When God sent His only son into the world to show them the Father through His miracles and ministry, they rejected Jesus; they crucified Him.

Good news! The Father raised Jesus up from the dead and Jesus ascended back into heaven. God created us for Himself; He placed us in a beautiful world; He gave us everything we could have possibly wanted or needed.

There is a tremendous spiritual battle going on; you need to know more about it and learn to **really** know who God is. This battle is not just about us; it is about Jesus Christ and His adversary, Satan.

Although God cast Satan and his angels, known to us as demons, out of heaven, God has permitted Satan to remain on the earth for a set period of time. Before Jesus was crucified Satan had access to heaven in order to talk to God. In the first two chapters of the book of Job it states that Satan appeared before God to discuss Job.

Satan is still our accuser today, but God looks on Jesus and is satisfied. Jesus made us holy; He justified us when we believed.

Here are some of the characteristics of Satan:
- ✓ Satan is a thief and destroyer, a murderer, a liar, a deceiver; he is very subtle and crafty.
- ✓ He is the father of everything evil.
- ✓ His greatest desire is to dethrone Jesus Christ.
- ✓ He is the enemy of anyone who follows Jesus Christ, and he tries to get as many followers away from Him as he can.
- ✓ He doesn't want God to have anyone to worship Him, and he is doing his best to destroy all that is good and decent in the world as part of this effort.

You need someone to hate? Hate evil and its spiritual perpetrators! Hating God will only put you in Satan's camp.

To avoid sin's tragedy learn Satan's strategy.

We are told about the final battle in the Book of Revelations. At that time Jesus will completely destroy Satan and his legions; Jesus will then rule and reign for eternity.

Sin will add to your trouble,
subtract from your energy,
and multiply your difficulties.

How can we recognize Satan?

Satan is a master of disguises, invisible ones, which makes it a bit difficult sometimes to figure out what is happening. He has the ability, if allowed or invited by any individual, to enter into a person's mind and take control.

History is full of such examples! The earth has been plagued ever since creation with evil people and leaders who have allowed Satan, knowingly for some and unknowingly for others, to control their lives.

The serpent in Eden was the first to permit Satan to use him and Satan hasn't quit since. He has all his demons trained to do the same thing!

hose whom he does not possess, he attacks. He does this by attacking the minds of unsuspecting victims, filling their heads full of lies that they often believe, causing them to leave the path of right and pattern their lifestyle more and more after Satan's.

These victims think they themselves are to blame, when all the time it is Satan's lies within them that are to blame!

They don't recognize that Satan is using their minds in an attempt to drive them away from God and into his own camp. Many of these victims, often little children, hear voices talking in their heads! These victims and their families don't know how to cope and react in different ways. In adults it can lead to drinking and drugs, even violence, in an effort to tune out these voices.

Some adults even believe they are losing their minds. This can lead to suicide, probably many more than we will ever know about.

Others react through nightmares; still others live in fear and terror without even having a real reason to do so. The more muddled and confused Satan can make our minds, the happier he is. People, in such a condition, aren't too much threat to him.

Satan cannot take a believer out of the hand of God but he can make a believer ineffective in ministry—that is his greatest threat to us.

If any of these things apply to you, it is not you that are to blame; it is Satan playing games with your mind. Don't give in to the lies he feeds you. Satan will fill you with doubt and fears; he will tell you that you are inferior, that nobody loves you. It is all lies! God loves you even if all your family, friends and acquaintances may not.

He made you; you are His creation and His plans for you are different than what others around you may think.

Learn to listen to God's voice and He will lead you in the path He has for you; He will be with you and give you the strength and grace to follow that path, no matter how hard it is.

God does not promise us an easy life, but we are not alone!

Listen to the struggle of Apostle Paul, a very godly man who ministered to believers in the early churches: "The law is good, then. The trouble is not with the law but with me, because I am sold into slavery, with sin as my master. I don't understand myself at all, for I really want to do what is right, but I don't do it.

Instead, I do the very thing I hate. I know perfectly well that what I am doing is wrong, and my bad conscience shows that I agree that the law is good. But I can't help myself, because it is sin inside me that makes me do these evil things.

"I know that I am rotten through and through so far as my old sinful nature is concerned. No matter which way I turn, I can't make myself do right. I want to, but I can't. When I want to do good, I don't. And when I try not to do wrong, I do it anyway. But if I am doing what I don't want to do, **I am not really the one doing it; the sin within me is doing it**.

"It seems to be a fact of life that when I want to do what is right, I inevitably do what is wrong. I love God's law with all my heart. But there is another law at work within me that is at war with my mind. This law wins the fight and makes me a slave to the sin that is still within me. Oh, what a miserable person I am! Who will free me from this life that is dominated by sin?

Thank God! The answer is in Jesus Christ our Lord. So you see how it is: In my mind I really want to obey God's law, but because of my sinful nature I am a slave to sin. Romans 7:14-25

Satan's goal is to separate you from God. He must prevent you from getting to know Jesus Christ at all costs! He can't stop you from being a Christian, but he can make you an ineffectual Christian. Remember—Satan is a strong adversary of God and he is determined to win. He is a poor loser; he will do anything he can to stop you from worshipping Jesus Christ. Satan does not fight fair, so beware!

The Christian walk is a battle, a spiritual warfare for your soul. God has given us the gift of free choice; He will not force us to love and worship Him.

There is good news! You can do something about it and win. God is on your side, even if you don't currently believe it. If you want God's help, all you have to do is ask for it. It is that simple. Remember that **you have access to God at all times**, no matter where you are! God is everywhere.

It doesn't take fancy prayers; just speak what is in your heart. You don't even have to talk to Him out loud; just commune with Him in your heart. He will hear you. Ask Him to forgive you; He will. Ask Him to guide and lead you; He will**, if you will let Him** and give Him the opportunity to do so. However, if you are making a declaration of faith, you want to do it out loud with conviction so that God is honored, you yourself, and others who hear you, are encouraged and Satan is rebuked.

You will be amazed at some of the changes for good that will begin to happen in your life. There is an inner joy and peace that you will enter into, once you seriously begin your relationship with Jesus Christ.

Just think...you will never be alone again! Jesus will never, never, never leave you alone, even if everyone else does. He will always be beside you and his Holy Spirit within you. You will become stronger in the Lord and more mature with each victory you gain. Your faith will build; your joy, peace and contentment will grow, even if the world around you is terrible and crumbling at your feet.

Apostle Paul tells us to be strong with the Lord's mighty power. We are to put on God's entire armor so that we will be able to stand firm against all strategies and tricks of the Devil. We are not fighting against people made of flesh and blood, but against the evil rulers and authorities of the unseen world, against those mighty powers of darkness who rule this world, and against wicked spirits in the heavenly realms.

We are to use every piece of God's armor to resist the enemy in the time of evil, so that after the battle we will still be standing firm. We must stand our ground, putting on the sturdy belt of truth and the body armor of God's righteousness. For shoes, we need to put on the peace that comes from the Good News, so that we will be fully equipped.

In every battle we will need faith as our shield to stop the fiery arrows aimed at us by Satan.

So we must put on salvation as our helmet, and take the sword of the Spirit, which is the word of God.

We should pray at all times and on every occasion in the power of the Holy Spirit. We need to stay alert and be persistent in our prayers for all Christians everywhere." See Ephesians 6:10-18.

Outward circumstances may or may not change, but the Holy Spirit will begin to give you wisdom and grace to enable you to overcome circumstances, no matter how bad they get. The Christian walk is not easy, but it is the only walk that can lead you to peace amidst the storms of life.

*If you flee from sin,
you won't fall into it.*

The quality of life and fulfillment now, and the eternal rewards later, make the struggle worthwhile. Sin blinds—but God's grace restores sight.

Sin prevented Adam and Eve and their descendants from being able to have a relationship with God. God had to find a way to restore this relationship with mankind. He made provision for a Redeemer, but that would not be for thousands of years later. He needed an answer for the then present day problem. This is when He required Adam and Eve to begin making animal sacrifices.

Why were animal sacrifices necessary?

The sacrificial lamb in the Old Testament was a type or forerunner of the crucifixion of Jesus Christ who was sacrificed on the cross for all the sins of mankind. Just as Jesus, in giving up His life, shed His blood, the animal sacrifice had to be complete - the animal had to die and in death shed its blood. That is the significance and importance of shed blood in sacrifice. Mankind could now have a relationship with God. The sacrifices served to remind God and man that the Redeemer for mankind was still coming.

The Old Testament believers looked forward to their salvation. The New Testament believers and every believer since then, look back to their Redeemer, Jesus Christ, after His death and resurrection. Therefore, animal **sacrifices are no longer needed; they would now be sacrilegious.**

Because of this we can now approach a holy and just God. God's love sees us through the sacrifice of His Son and can accept us because Jesus has taken all the sins of the world upon His own shoulders to make this possible for us. However, **we must still choose Him** before this applies to us. The provision is there; it is up to us to accept it.

If we do not accept it, by default we are rejecting it.

When Jesus died on the cross, the curtain protecting the Holy of Holies was torn into two parts!

The Father made a statement—everybody could now have direct personal access to God without any other mediator; a human priest was no longer necessary. The ultimate sacrifice had already been made—the death of Jesus Christ. The Father raised Him up from the dead, and Jesus now reigns in heaven with His heavenly Father.

When Jesus left this earth, He said he would send the Comforter to be with us until His return to get us. He did that; the Comforter is the Holy Spirit. It is the Holy Spirit that comes to live within us at our conversion. The Holy Spirit regenerates us, instructs us, and empowers us.

He fills us full of the joy and peace of the Lord and sustains us. He watches over us in times of stress and trouble. We need to learn to listen to Him when He communicates with us; He will never force himself upon us.

What reciprocated the first murder?

Adam and Eve lived for a long time after they were sent out of the garden. They had many sons and daughters during those years. Adam died when he was 930 years old. Cain and Abel were the first two children born to Adam and Eve outside the Garden of Eden. Cain was a farmer and Abel was a shepherd.

Both Cain and Abel knew that animal sacrifices were necessary on a regular basis in order to commune with God.

They both knew all the rules regarding sacrifices, because they were grown men at the time of Cain's dispute with God, and they would have been well taught by Adam in regard to sacrifices and their purpose.

One day when it was time for the sacrifice both Cain and Abel presented their sacrifices before God.

Cain presented God with the first fruits from his garden and Abel sacrificed a lamb. God accepted Abel's sacrifice, but He rejected Cain's. God instructed Cain to get a lamb and sacrifice it as Abel had done. He gave him a chance to do it right.

However, this made Cain mad. Cain told Abel what God had said, then in a jealous rage Cain killed Abel and buried him in a field.

God's swift judgment followed. God placed a curse on Cain. The land would no longer produce crops for him, and he would become a wanderer and a vagrant upon the earth. Cain told God that he was **afraid that his relatives would kill him** for what he had done, so God placed a mark on Cain.

God told everyone that anyone killing Cain would receive God's vengeance seven-fold.

It would seem that there were already many other brothers and sisters around, not just Adam and Eve! Some day we will know for sure.

Where did Cain get his wife?

Traditional View

There were many daughters born to Adam and Eve as well as more sons. The Bible does not give us any hint as to when any of the daughters were born. It only mentions more sons and daughters in the genealogy.

Since Adam was 130 years old when Seth, his third son, was born, it is quite possible that many daughters had been born in between and after Cain and Abel were born. In those days they married sisters since there was no one else. Cain could have been over 100 years old when Seth was born!

Cain may have already been married when he killed Abel. His wife would have gone with him when he left. If not, he could have married one of his sisters or cousins many years later. They lived to be hundreds of years old in the beginning; they were so healthy.

He settled down eventually in the land of Nod where some of his relatives were also settled. His firstborn son was Enoch. Cain built a city and named it Enoch after his first son. His city would have been filled with relatives. The Bible gives his lineage for many generations. Many talented people were among the descendants of Cain.

Seth, the third son of Adam and Eve, was the son whose descendants continued down through the years until the birth of Jesus Christ. See Luke 3.

Second View

Many theologians insist that the "sons of God" mentioned in this section refers to fallen angels that married the sons and daughters of Adam. Perhaps Cain married one of them.

There were giants in the land at that time, and it is believed that these giants were the result of the union between angels and humans.

God was very angry that the "sons of God" had intermarried with humans.

There is no scriptural basis that I can find to support this theory. In Matthew 22:30 Jesus said (speaking about resurrected believers), "For when the dead rise they won't be married. They will be like the angels in heaven." The Holy Bible says angels don't marry in heaven, so why would they come down on earth and marry here?

Third View

If the "sons of God" were not angels, then who were they?

The Bible provides no time frame. Adam and Eve possibly lived in Eden for many years before committing the sin of eating the forbidden fruit. God had told Adam and Eve to be fruitful and multiply, and they would have obeyed this mandate from God.

The number of years they would have had in the garden before their "fall" is unknown. God does not give us that information. There could have been many children born while they were in the garden. These children would definitely have been considered the "sons of God." They would **not** have been born in sin, so they would not be sent into exile with Adam and Eve. In the New Testament believers are often called the "sons of God." See John 1:12; Romans 8:15-17, 29.

When Adam and Eve sinned and were sent out of Eden, their children would not have been forced to leave because they did not sin and were not born in sin.

However, the Bible says that when some of the "sons of God" saw that the daughters of Adam (born after the fall) were beautiful, they chose to leave the garden and began to intermarry with them.

One of the possible results of these intermarriages was the birth of giants, strong and mighty men. Not all of the sons of God would have sinned this way. The ones who did, and all their offspring, would have been destroyed during the flood, along with everyone else. The ones who didn't sin would have been removed to heaven or could still be in Eden, which could just be hidden from us. They would continue to reproduce since they were not in a sinless state and would never die.

There is one scripture that could support this aspect of this theory. In the first two chapters of Job it states that Satan joined the "sons of God" to appear before God. Satan was there to talk to God about Job. In the beginning of the second chapter the "sons of God" are once more presenting themselves before the Lord, and Satan joins them once again.

Angels are always coming and going before the Lord to worship him, but the "sons of God" seemed to have set times when they appeared before God to commune with Him.

The big question is, "who **were** the 'sons of God?" One thing to remember when you are studying subjects like this one, there is no way that any person can prove one way or the other who these "sons of God" were. We will find out when we get to heaven.

Don't try to make a big issue out of this. God didn't consider it important enough to tell us, so we don't need to make it an important issue either. I have included it in this book as a point of interest and something to think about, nothing more.

The main reason God tells us so much about the first three sons born **after** the "fall of Adam and Eve" is to provide the history and genealogy of Jesus Christ, our Messiah and Redeemer. Beyond that it states that many more sons and daughters were born to them. No more information is given.

Summary

After God rested from His creating, two major events took place, changing life on earth forever.

The first was the fall of man when Adam and Eve ate of the forbidden fruit and the second was the first murder when Cain killed Abel.

There are some people who believe we are still living in the seventh day because God is no longer creating. Who knows? I guess it all depends on which Creation Theory you believe as to where we are now. It doesn't really matter; if it did, God would have given us a more thorough explanation. What does matter is the truths that God has given us in the Bible.

History is still unfolding; we will just have to wait and see what is going to happen. There are many prophecies about the end times and just as many different interpretations. That doesn't really matter either.

What you have to keep in mind is that Jesus Christ is coming back for His Church and when He does, will you be a member? I am praying that every reader of this book will be there, and I am looking forward to meeting you all and hearing your stories once we are all together with Jesus Christ.

In creation we see God's hand;
in redemption we see his heart.
The wonders of creation point
to our wonderful Creator!

Notes:

Chapter Four

Degeneration and Destruction of Mankind

HOW BIG WAS THE ARK

The ark was not designed to be steered to a destination; it was designed to withstand a global flood. It did not need a pointed front or steering mechanism of any kind, but was built for solidarity and to provide space for animals and people God was saving to start the new world when the flood ended.

Noah's Ark was taller than a 3-story building and had three interior decks each deck being the size of thirty-six (36) lawn tennis courts

Its length was 300 cubits (450 feet or 135 meters); its width was 50 cubits (75 feet or 22.5 meters; its height was 30 cubits (45 feet, or 13.5 meters).

It could have been larger because longer cubits may have been used. In those days a cubic was the length of a man's arm from fingertips to elbow. The question is, "How long was Moses' arm?" (Moses is considered to be the writer of Genesis.) Over the years 18 inches became the standard for a cubit. No matter how you look at it, this ark was very huge!

The ark was basically a rectangle with the sides and ends sloping out. Because the sides sloped out at the top, each deck was a little wider than the one below it. Narrow window openings went all along the top to provide ventilation and light. The windows were about 18 square, no glass! All the windows had shutters.

The ark was built to withstand raging oceans; it only had to float, it did not have to go anywhere! It would have been quite low in the water due to its heavy cargo of animals, people and their food supplies and would have been almost impossible to overturn. God gave Noah all the instructions for building the ark. It took Noah and his sons one hundred years to complete. They had to make all their own lumber by hand. They and all the animals survived over a year of flood waters before they could leave the ark!

Large stone anchors have been discovered which must have hung from the bottom of the ark to provide stability.

Chapter 4—Degeneration and Destruction of Mankind

Who was Noah?

In Genesis 6:7-8 we are told of the fast decline of the spiritual and moral life of the descendants of Adam and Eve.

" Now the Lord looked about upon the earth and observed the extent of the people's wickedness; he saw that all their thoughts were consistently and totally evil, so the Lord was sorry he had ever made them. It broke his heart.

"And the Lord said, 'I will completely wipe out this human race that I have created. Yes, and I will destroy all the animals and birds, too. I am sorry I ever made them.' But **Noah found favor with the Lord**." (Bold is mine.)

There was grace even in the Old Testament before the Savior, Jesus, came.

All the patriarchs of this time lived for hundreds of years, giving birth to many sons and daughters. However, among all the thousands of people now upon the earth, God could only find one man, Noah, and his immediate family, who still worshipped God.

Noah was a descendant of Seth. At this time Noah was 500 years old.

God instructed Noah and his sons to build an ark that would hold his family and one pair of every ceremonial unclean animals and seven of each ceremonial clean animals, plus the birds of the air. The clean animals were animals designated as clean by God for use in sacrifices, so they needed more of them.

They built the ark according to God's specifications. During the time of building, many people ridiculed them because they were building a big ship in the middle of dry land, but Noah, in spite of their criticism and mocking, did as God had told him to do.

Up to this time there still had been no rain on the earth, for the earth was still watered at night by the dew rising from the ground, so Noah's claims of rains and a universal flood caused great mirth among the people.

When the ark was completed and all their provisions were loaded onto the ark, God had all the animals and birds approach the ark and enter, then Noah and his family entered and God sealed the door shut.

The Universal Flood

The rains began. It rained extremely hard for forty days and forty nights. The water rose higher and higher. The earth sank lower and lower as the waters beneath the crust of earth broke through to the surface.

Ark during the first 40 days - An artist's conception

When the torrential rains and the underground fountains stopped, the water was 25 feet (7.7 meters) above the highest point of land.

The breakup of the earth's crust caused all kinds of new valleys and mountains to evolve. Creation scientists believe that many of the very high mountain ranges of today were much lower before the flood.

The volcanoes and earthquakes caused by the eruption of the earth's crust would have caused enormous changes to the landscape. Creation scientists have written many good books on this subject for those wishing to know more about the flood and its resultant aftermath.

The water subsided slowly over the next year until, finally, the ark came to rest upon the top of the mountains of Ararat as the waters receded. Noah and his family and all the birds and animals left the ark and began to spread out across the world, as their numbers increased, for God had told them to multiply and be fruitful upon the earth.

Upon leaving the ark Noah and his family built an altar and sacrificed to God, giving thanks to Him for rescuing them all from the flood. God created a spectacular rainbow to glow across the whole sky. God told them that from that time forward the rainbow would be a constant reminder to man that God would never again destroy the world with a universal flood.

The rainbow was a symbol of God's covenant with mankind. Once again mankind began to multiply upon the earth.

A new beginning

God watched the humans He had created; once more they were becoming independent and Godless. See Genesis 11.

He could not again destroy the human race with a flood because of His covenant with Noah and his family, but He was very displeased.

Even before the flood God officially shortened man's days to 120 years so that they would not have so much opportunity to become evil. He had said, "My Spirit will not put up with humans for such a long time, for they are only mortal flesh. In the future, they will live no more than 120 years." Genesis 6:3

Many still lived much longer than that but not as old as any of the old patriarchs. However, it did not stop evil from once again spreading like a plague throughout the earth after the flood.

Tower of Babel

Only a few short verses in Genesis 11 discuss the "Tower of Babel," but it is an very important subject. Over the last few decades a great deal of light has been shed on this Biblical account and the discoveries have shown how accurate this account is.

Artist conception by Marten van Valckenborch, circa 1660

According to the Biblical account the people were living in close proximity instead of spreading out throughout the world like God had told them to do. At that point in time they all spoke a universal language. As a result, they were able to communicate with one another.

In Genesis 9:1 God had said, "Be fruitful and multiply, and replenish the earth."

However, the people had a different idea. In Genesis 11:4 we read, "Come," they said, "let's make great piles of burnt brick and collect natural asphalt to use as mortar.

Let's build a great city with a tower that reaches to the skies - a monument to our greatness! This will bring us together and keep us from scattering all over the world."

This city was to the east and was located in the plains of Shinar. They were seeking fame and fortune and wanted to rule themselves. God was completely left out of their plans.

Foreign gods and idols became widespread.

God looked down from heaven upon this city and said, "Come, let's go down and give them different languages. Then they won't be able to understand each other." Genesis 11:7

This God did. "The Lord scattered them all over the earth," verse 9. God separated them into family groups and He placed them in different locations of the world according to their languages.

Those who were still in the area stopped building the city. God called the city Babel, "...because it was there that the Lord confused the people by giving them many languages," verse 9.

In chapter 10:32, after listing the genealogies of Noah and his sons, the Bible says, "These are the families that came from Noah's sons, **listed nation by nation**, according to their lines of descent. The earth was populated with people of these nations after the flood.

Point of Interest

I am including this next section in my book to help those of you who may have serious doubts about the reality of a world flood.

Perhaps what you read here will help you to realize the truth of everything that is recorded in the Holy Bible. Some of the following information is taken from Anchor Stones web site.[16]

Below the mountainous region in Northeast Turkey, where the ark finally settled, was a large plain in the "land of Shinar." There are no firm boundaries known for the "land of Shinar," however, somewhere on this plain they built the Tower of Babel. The Bible says they used baked brick, using slime (bitumen, tar, and asphalt) for mortar. Samples from a large tell in this area revealed a very black mortar that consisted of a mixture of sand and tar which hardens when dried. This was a petroleum product! The Tower of Babel could have been right in this area. No one knows for certain...yet.

Research and excavations are continually bringing new information to light. The modern Babylon is not necessarily Babel.

The 1985 Encyclopedia Britannica states that the only oil fields in Turkey are in Ramona and Gaziantep both less than 100 miles from the site of this particular tell the approximate or most likely area for the Tower of Babel to be located. The presence of oil here 4,000 years after the time of Babel indicates that an ample supply of bitumen most likely could have been obtained by the builders of this infamous city and tower. It may have been a major reason for selecting this site.

When the people began to migrate from the Ararat region, they **banded together** to avoid being scattered. Evidence of ancient history all points to the fact that the earliest of people had rejected God. They wanted to worship other gods and make a name for themselves by building a city with a massive tower reaching into the heavens. Just 400 years after the flood.

Such a building project needed many thousands of bricks and lots of mortar to hold them together. Noah and his sons were from the pre-flood world, a world whose people most certainly possessed knowledge and technology equal to much of what we know today. At least some of this knowledge would have been passed on to their immediate descendants.

Probably the only thing that prevented a very advanced civilization from erupting was the fact that they had to concentrate on breeding animals and cultivating crops that would sustain their lives. They had lost everything in the flood!

With every great mind on earth together in one accord and of one language, they could have done many great and wonderful things! But they turned their backs on God, and God thwarted their plans.

When Noah and his family left the ark, they had knowledge. What they didn't have were the resources to put that knowledge to work.

When God came down and gave all the family groupings different languages, there would have been utter chaos!

They could no longer communicate with one another! The building of the city and tower was stopped, and they were forced to scatter abroad as God had commanded. There is now compelling evidence that shows that it was indeed this very area in Turkey that the different languages of the world originated.

By the time Abraham went to Canaan 427 years after the flood, we know that the different nations were already established in their lands. 427 years isn't a very long time in the overall scheme of things.

However, take a look at how our country has grown and the various stages it went through in just the last 150 to 200 years! Add to that the fact that people in those days did not die young, and they all had large families. They migrated and spread over the face of the earth by the thousands!

It is believed that Babel occurred around 150 to 175 years after the flood (2198-2148BC). This is based on how long it would have taken to have enough people to scatter abroad!

Excavators in the region have found evidence which shows that Mt. Ararat, the "traditional" site of the ark, was not formed until many, many years after the flood. In excavations of early settlements in the region of eastern and central Turkey, in the **region** which was once called "Ararat," many tools and other objects have been found in and by volcanoes. Because of the unique trace elements found in obsidian, it is possible to match specimens found in settlements with sources whose obsidian exhibit's the same trace element.

These analyses show that the earliest settlements in this region obtained their obsidian from Nemrut Dag, the volcano on the north side of Lake Van, about 70 miles south of Mt. Ararat. They would not have traveled that far if it had been available from Mt. Ararat. Mt. Ararat had to have been formed by later volcanoes.

Our current civilization all began in Turkey. Turkey has so many site significant archaeology that no one has been able to count them! An estimated guess is that there are some 40,000 sites, ranging from scattered burials to the remains of magnificent cities! The great majority of these sites are in unpoliced rural areas, many of them only recently opened up by the building of roads.

The area where the ark came to rest was in a mountain range just a few miles south of the Araxes Valley or Ararat Plain.

The Aras (Araxes) River runs through this valley, beginning in Erzurum, Turkey - west of Noah's home - and flowing east, it then forms part of the Turkish-Russian and Turkish-Iranian border. The two volcanic Ararat mountains arose in this plain and can be seen from the presumed site of the ark as arising abruptly from the green, fertile valley.

This whole area possesses a special fertility that is indicative of the special provisions God made for the first family in re-establishing life on this planet. Even to this day vegetables grown in the area near the presumed site of the ark are exceptionally large!

In Genesis 6:21 we read that God instructed Noah to gather food products into the ark for both themselves and all the animals. This would have included seeds for planting. Once they left the ark they began to sow the seeds that would produce food. Archaeological excavations reveal evidences that fit this scenario perfectly.

In this part of Turkey there are many varieties of timber available for building. More important yet, there are many species of edible plants, the most important being cereals.

This is problematic for archaeologists because of the unsolved questions of origins. Noah's flood is the only answer that explains this adequately!

It was in Turkey that many plants were "reborn," planted there by Noah and his family from seeds brought there from before the flood. From there they were carried to various parts of the world. Recent work has shown a large percentage of plants are endemic, that is, confined to Turkey. This is exciting, because it means that there are a large number of plants that are found **only in Turkey**!

When the people migrated from Turkey, they only took with them the major grain and staple plant foods, leaving behind a variety of plants whose beginnings were in the pre-flood world.

They also had many varieties of fruit, which is amazing, considering the cold climate of the northeastern and central part of Turkey. To this day Turkey has fruits that thrive in spite of its cold climate! Apples, plums, apricots, peaches and mulberries are common in the eastern highlands.

In Genesis 9:20 the Bible states that Noah planted a vineyard. Vineyards are usually found in warm climates! Today, in this cold region of Turkey, the vine is a hardy plant.

To sum up the evidences, the earliest specimens and forms of many, many plant foods are found in the ancient settlements extending outward from the area of the ark and even the possible site for Babel.

Even today Turkey has plants found nowhere else in the world! **There is no explanation for this except the Genesis account.**

A few miles from the site of the ark, in the Araxes Valley, is a vast complex of extremely ancient stone fences radiating outward from a very ancient stone house. Behind this complex (to the north) is a stone altar located upon a ridge between two hills. In front of this house are two tombstones that indicated they are marking the graves of Noah and his wife.

It is reasonable to believe this indicates that this was Noah's house.

Within a few miles of Noah's home is what has been termed "one of," if not "THE" oldest metallurgical site ever found! Analyses of copper found there showed 14 different alloys, including tin, lead, antimony and zinc. The sophistication of this metalworking center has fascinated archaeologists. They claim it is "indeed unique in its complexity and long life."

They found clay pipes inserted in the furnaces for use with bellows. They also found the first phase of phosphorus briquettes. Phosphorus was used in the smelting of cassiterite to obtain tin.

They also found another ancient metalworking center in the Araxes Valley. It is reasonable to believe that the immediate descendants of Noah were those who had the earliest knowledge of metallurgy and employed it from the beginning.

Archaeologists have found very few metal objects in this valley. There is evidence that the people migrated from this valley and were not forced out by enemies or by nature. Since metal was a precious commodity, it would never have been left behind. Pottery was heavy and easily obtainable, so some always got left behind when the people moved to a new area.

Not metal. Old or worn out objects could be melted down and new products made or formed.

In Genesis 4 we read about the descendants of Cain. One of them, Jubal, was the inventor of the harp and the flute! He was the first to work with metal, forging instruments of bronze and iron. This was many years before the flood; they already had bronze then! Is it surprising to find that Noah and his family knew metallurgy? It had already been around for hundreds of years before the flood!

In later years invading armies confiscated metal objects. Much of that was probably melted down and new items produced. Scholars have a tendency to try and explain evidences in the light of their own theories, most of which do **not** include the Biblical account.

These peoples did not come to this valley from somewhere else in the world. They came from Noah and his family, the sole survivors of the flood. God had the ark settle in this area for a reason! Evidence indicates that this Araxes Valley is the "original" home from which this culture subsequently expanded in all directions.

There is evidence that the next hazard Noah and his family faced in the following years was the sudden growth of wild, carnivorous animals, such as lions and tigers. Many of these varieties increase in litters at a rapid rate. There would have been a need to protect their herds and families from these predators. This would explain the need for the high stone fences found in this area.

In some of the towns houses have been found that were built without any doors! They climbed a ladder to the roof and descended into the house from there. Another way to keep out the wild animals?

In some cases houses have been built tight together with a central courtyard and only one exit to the outside. Many homes showed that their dead were buried under a stone slab within their houses, possibly to protect them from the wild animals?

In Exodus 23:29, God says, "I will not drive them the Hittite and the Canaanite out from before them in one year; lest the land become desolate, **and the beasts of the field multiply against thee**."

It is obvious that there were many wild animals in the area just waiting to take over the conquered lands. The Israelites did not have a big enough population in the beginning to protect the land and keep out the wild animals.

In Turkey there are still many wild animals lurking about in the mountains.

Also, in Turkey they found teeth and other fragments from the skeletons of hippopotamus, alphas antiquus (an extinct type of elephant), horse, cave bear and hyena. These were not fossils; they were post-flood animals. Noah's family and descendants had much more to contend with than we could possibly imagine! Obviously, not all of the animals dispersed around the world at any great speed. It must have been a slow migration in every direction from Turkey. Meanwhile, they threatened the people in numerous ways.

It was during this time that Nimrod (Genesis 10:8-9), the mighty hunter, made his claim to fame. Many tales of Nimrod's exploits have been passed down through history and some are still talked about today! The Bible talks about him as well. The mighty hunters of this period were a necessity. They had to control the wild animals that were increasing rapidly all around them.

Their herds and families were in jeopardy. Nimrod was the most famous of these mighty hunters.

The first major migration from Noah's area was the group that decided to build a big city and a tower that could reach to the heavens. We have already discussed the results of this particular migration.

With the confusion of the languages many people began to communicate through pictures, pictures even a child could understand! In time many would have begun to learn some of the other languages near them, but in the beginning there would have been utter chaos. None of their languages were in a written form until much later.

After Babel where did all the people go? Family groups had the same language.

The logical thing to do would be to establish towns and cities for each language group. They would need room for homes, crops and animals, so it would have been necessary to spread out in many directions. There is evidence that some left the area completely, while others settled down not too far away.

Because they were separated, not every family group would have all the skills that were available when they were all together!

Each town now took on a new character of its own as each group built to suit their own needs and within their own skills and abilities. These homes weren't primitive. Common building practices included wooden frames with mud bricks, then plastered with mortar. Many times they show evidences of having been replastered many, many times, much like we would paint our homes when they begin to flake.

At one site, when the archaeologists reached the earliest level, they found almost no pottery, leading them to believe these people were primitive and used no eating utensils. Then they discovered carbonized wooden dishes and vessels along with basketry.

Another thing of interest to archaeologists is the fact that all of these towns show some signs of skill in metallurgy. They had dated all these towns at different times, but the similarity in so many areas has created problems and brought confusion into some of their reasoning. They **were** all from the same time period...the answer true and simple. The Biblical account explains this quite clearly. Many archaeologists don't want to accept the Biblical account of the flood, so it is very difficult for them to puzzle these things out in another way.

They found obsidian beads with such small holes drilled through them that a modern steel needle cannot go through the hole. How did they do that? Obviously, the people who occupied these towns were very knowledgeable. In spite of the means we have today, they would probably have put us all to shame!

In all of these earliest settlements there is no evidence of invaders. It appears that they lived here for a while, then packed up and moved on to somewhere else. Evidence also exists everywhere that these people were worshipping false gods.

After the early peoples left Turkey, we know they eventually scattered all over the world.

There have been completely unknown civilizations that have come to light. I shall mention just one of them, Mohenjo Daro, because this city has been so well preserved that you could move into it and live there today! This discovery was in the Indus Valley.

These cities were built from baked brick - not sun dried brick. They must have burnt up a lot of trees to make these cities.

That may be why they eventually had to move on to somewhere else. They would have run out of available trees after a while. It would be easier to go to a new area and start again.

These cities used advanced construction, complete with drainage systems, underground water mains and bathrooms in every house! All these things have been so well preserved, they could be used today, including the indoor bathrooms. It is suspected that this advanced knowledge of waste-disposal came from one who had expert knowledge of the subject after living with seven other people over a year in a ship filled with animals of every kind!

Roads had been found covered with a sort of Macadam made of fragments of pottery and bits of crushed brick, soaked and tamped, probably to avoid the dust and mud which are the scourge of Far Eastern towns.

Their waste disposal system was remarkably well made and cleverly designed. Primitives? I don't think so!

There is evidence that the people of this city also raised wheat, melons, barley, dates and **cotton.** They fished the river with nets. They raised cattle, sheep, pigs and poultry. Their craftsmen made statuettes and figurines of such quality that one would think they came from Greece over 1000 years later. They fashioned elaborate jewelry of gold, silver, copper, shell and stone.

They had auger drills, household utensils and toilets; pottery painted and plain, hand-turned and turned on the wheel; terra cotta, dice and chess-men; coins older than any previously known; faience work of excellent quality (earthenware decorated with opaque colored glazes); stone carving superior to that of the Sumerians; copper weapons and implements, and a copper model of a two-wheeled cart; gold and silver bangles, ear-ornaments, necklaces, and other jewelry that were so well finished and so beautifully polished that they might have come out of a Bond Street jeweler's of today rather than from a prehistoric house of 5,000 years ago.

The women even had lipstick, eye makeup which is still used today (kohl) and perfume! The excavators also found red ochre used for lips and cheeks!

One particular piece of ochre, worn on one end, was found laying on a small low table beside vases of kohl, flasks of perfume, hairpins and bronze razors.

There was even evidence that there were cats and dogs as pets.

Their writing was mostly in forms of pictures. About four hundred different pictures or signs have been identified so far. There is no known language to compare it with, so experts cannot begin to interpret what these signs mean.

Their pictures give evidence of the animals that were in the area at the time. Pictures of monkeys, hares, doves, tigers, bears, rhinoceros, parrots, deer and great humped cattle. Since no monkeys or parrots live in this barren wasteland today, this is good evidence that this valley was once a jungle land.

One major difference in this city from others found is the absence of any temples. There were no signs of religion at all, so it is difficult to determine what they believed.

Some of the pictures they found resemble the later gods of the Hindu religion, which are similar to those found in other parts of the world.

They also found a coffin that was made of six thin superimposed layers of wood with the grain alternating as in modern plywood!

Modern man believes that optical lenses and eyeglasses are an invention of the last 400 to 500 years. Yet, there is evidence that early man had these devices long, long ago.

In fact it appears that these were so common and everyday that little was thought about the importance of writing about them.

But in time, knowledge of these devices grew less and less until it was lost until man "reinvented" the idea over 1,000 years after the last historical mention of them.

In the edge of the mountains of Lebanon, over 2,300 feet above sea level is Baalbek. The existing remains are the most astounding every found, a hewn stone, 68 feet by 14 feet. These ancient builders not only chiseled out these huge stones, but they moved them!

Today, even with our sophisticated engineering methods, it is doubtful that we could even lift stones like this, not to mention transporting them to their final location and lifting them into place.

We know they did. The obelisks of ancient Egypt and the pyramids prove that they did it. Engineers of today still haven't determined how it was done! Serious scientists and scholars remain silent on subjects such as this because they are unable to explain them.

There are many other discoveries that I could write about, but I think I have made my point. Only the Biblical account of Noah and the ark and the tower of Babel can explain or make sense of all the things that have been discovered.

I hope this diversion into archaeology has helped to put to rest any doubts you might have had about the flood and Babel being real!

This completes the background material for the rest of the book. I have attempted to show how God has dealt with mankind from Adam and Eve up to and right after the flood and the Tower of Babel. He is still dealing with mankind today, but His methods are not quite as obvious as they were back in the Old Testament times. However, God has not changed and His principles and laws are still in effect today.

Chapter Five

God's Plan for Your Life

*Salvation is so simple we can overlook it,
so profound <u>we</u> can never accomplish it.*

Chapter 5—God's Plan of Salvation

If you do not belong to a good church family of any kind, I would strongly recommend that you find a church where there is life happening and become a part of a group of Christian believers.

Hebrews 10:25 says, "And let us not neglect our meeting together, as some people do, but encourage and warn each other, especially now that the day of His coming back again is drawing near."

We all need someone to pray for us and to help us along the Christian path and we, in turn, need to minister to others.

Eternal Life

God loves you and wants you to experience His peace and life.

The Bible says:

"For God so loved the world that he gave his only Son, so that everyone who believes in him will not perish but have eternal life. God did not send his Son into the world to condemn it, but to save it." John 3:16, 17

Union with God—Not Separation

By nature man is separated from God.

The Bible says:

"For all have sinned; all fall short of God's glorious standard." Romans 3:23

God's Remedy is the Cross

God's love bridges the gap of separation between God and you. Jesus paid the penalty for your sins when He died on the cross and rose from the grave.

The Bible says:

"He personally carried away our sins in His own body on the cross so we can be dead to sin and live for what is right. You have been healed by His wounds." I Peter 2:24

Man's Response is to Receive Christ

You cross the gap into God's family when you receive Christ as your personal Savior.

The Bible says:

> "But to all who believed Him and accepted Him,
> He gave the right to become children of God." John 1:12

Prayer of Commitment

You can receive Christ right now by faith through prayer. God knows your heart and is not so concerned with your words as He is with your attitude. Prayer is talking with God. A sample prayer follows. If this prayer expresses the desire in your heart, then you can use it as your prayer right now:

"Lord Jesus, I know I am a sinner. I need you. I believe you died for my sins. Right now, I turn from my sins and open the door of my life and receive You as my Savior and Lord. Thank you for forgiving my sins and giving me eternal life. I give you control of my life. Make me the kind of person You want me to be. Help me to fulfill my destiny. Amen."

Where Do I Go From Here?

You need to begin to grow in your relationship with Christ. You do this by talking to Him. Pray about everything. Pray specifically and pray honestly. God talks to you through the Bible—it is your spiritual food. Read it daily. Without spiritual food, you will become weak and sickly in your spiritual life.

Share your new life with other people. This is witnessing. This comes about as a natural result of growing spiritually.

Finally, find other believers who can help you and with whom you can fellowship. If possible, attend a Bible study class where you can ask questions and continue to grow into spiritual maturity.

FOLLOWING ARE SOME SCRIPTURES TO HELP YOU:

When Afflicted:
Psalm 119:67, 71, 75 - often providential
Psalm 34:19 -- God will deliver

When Anxious:
Philippians 4:6, 7 - relieved through prayer
I Peter 5:7 - God cares for you

When Discouraged:
Galatians 6:9 - don't give up
Isaiah 41:10 -- God will strengthen and help

When Doubting:
John 3:16 - eternal life promised
I John 5:11-13 -- you can be sure

When Lonely:
Hebrews 13:5, 6 - His presence promised
Psalm 16:11 - joy in His presence

When Worried:
Philippians 4:19 - God will provide
I John 5:14, 15 - claim His promises
Hebrews 13:5, 6 - will never forsake you

REFERENCES

1. *Cry Joy* by Jerry Mercer, Victor Books

2. *The Heart of George MacDonald* by George MacDonald. Deceased.

3. Nicky Gumbel from the Alpha Course Tapes
   http://www.alphacourse.org

4. #Y137. The Theory of Creation – An analysis of the Biblical Creation Story by Jim Schicatano
   Information gleaned from his web site article, which is based on his book. www.yfiles.com/Biblical-creation.htm

5. The Uniqueness of Creation Week by Lambert Dolphin
   http://www.ldolphin.org/Unique.html

6. The Literal Interpretation of the Genesis One Creation Account by Rich Deem
   http://www.godandscience.org/youngearth/genesis.html

7. A Look at Creation Theories, Past and Present
   http://sci.uncletom2000.com/creation.htm

8. Information gleaned from the web site www.adamictimeline.com

9. Bible Numerics – The Work of Dr. Ivan Panin. Deceased.
   Information gleaned from the web site
   http://www.sigler.org/finnestad/bible.htm

10. Bible Numerics by Jerry Chin - He uses Ivan Panin's Book called, "The Inspiration of the Hebrew Scriptures Scientifically Demonstrated," published by The Book Society of Canada Ltd., Agincourt, Ontario.

    http://www.accessv.com/~rjchin/numeric/exodus/genesis.htm

11. Freedom from Fear by D.G. Clark. Deceased. Sussex, England.

12. *Wild at Heart* by John Eldredge, Page 133

13. Larry Randolph – Audio tape

    From sermon preached at New Life Vineyard, Kelowna, BC on June 9, 1996, Friday P.M. #426

    http://www.larryrandolph.com

14. *Six Hours One Friday* by Max Lucado, Multnomah Publishers, Inc.

15. *Intercessory Prayer* by Dutch Sheets

    http://dutchsheets.org

16. Anchor Stones, Wyatt Archaeological Discoveries

    http://anchorstone.com/

17. The International Standard Bible Encyclopaedia, Eerdmans

18. *The Case for Creation* by Lee Stobel, Zondervan

19. Stephen C. Meyer - Interviewed by Lee Stobel

20. Short History of Nearly Everything, Bill Bryson quoted by Lee Stobel
21. William Lane Craig - Interviewed by Lee Stobel
22. *Climbing Mount Parable*, Richard Dawkins - Quoted by Lee Strobel
23. *The Bondage Breaker* by Neil T. Anderson, Harvest House

RECOMMENDED READING

1. *Cry Joy* by Jerry L. Mercer, Victor Books

2. *Intercessory Prayer* by Dutch Sheets, Regal

3. *Wild At Heart* by John Eldredge, Thomas Nelson Publishers

4. *Victory Over The Darkness* by Neil T. Anderson, Regal

5. *The Bondage Breaker* by Neil T. Anderson, Regal

6. *Waking the Dead* by John Eldredge, Thomas Nelson Publishers

7. *Fight Like A Man* by Gordon Dalby, Word Publishing

8. *Healing the Masculine Soul* by Gordon Dalby, Word Publishing

9. The Unshakable Kingdom And The Unchanging Person by E. Stanley Jones, Abingdon Press

10. *Six Hours One Friday* by Max Lucado, Multnomah Publishers, Inc.

11. The Normal Christian Life by Watchman Nee

12. *The Spiritual Man* by Watchman Nee, Christian Fellowship Publishers, Inc.

13. *Waking the Dead* by John Eldredge, Thomas Nelson Publishers

14 *The Case for Creation* by Lee Strobel, Zandervan Publishers.

15 *The Heart of George McDonald* by George McDonald. Deceased.

Made in the USA
Charleston, SC
28 May 2016